Force of the Heart:

Tango, Art

Mộng Lan 2011

Force of the Heart:
Tango, Art

Mộng-Lan

Force of the Heart: Tango, Art

ISBN: 978-0-9828227-0-8

Printed in the United States of America

First paperback edition, 2011

Published by

Valiant Press

P.O. Box 2771

Sugar Land, Texas 77487

Cover painting, Mộng-Lan, *Tango in Red,* acrylic on canvas, 70 cm x 100 cm, 2011

Cover photograph, cover and text design by Mộng-Lan

Poem, "Esperándote (Waiting for You)" by Mộng-Lan

www.monglan.com

Other books by Mộng-Lan

Song of the Cicadas

Why is the Edge Always Windy?

Love Poem to Tofu & Other Poems (poems & art, chapbook)

Tango, Tangoing: Poems & Art

Tango, Tangueando: Poemas & Dibujos (bilingual Spanish-English edition)

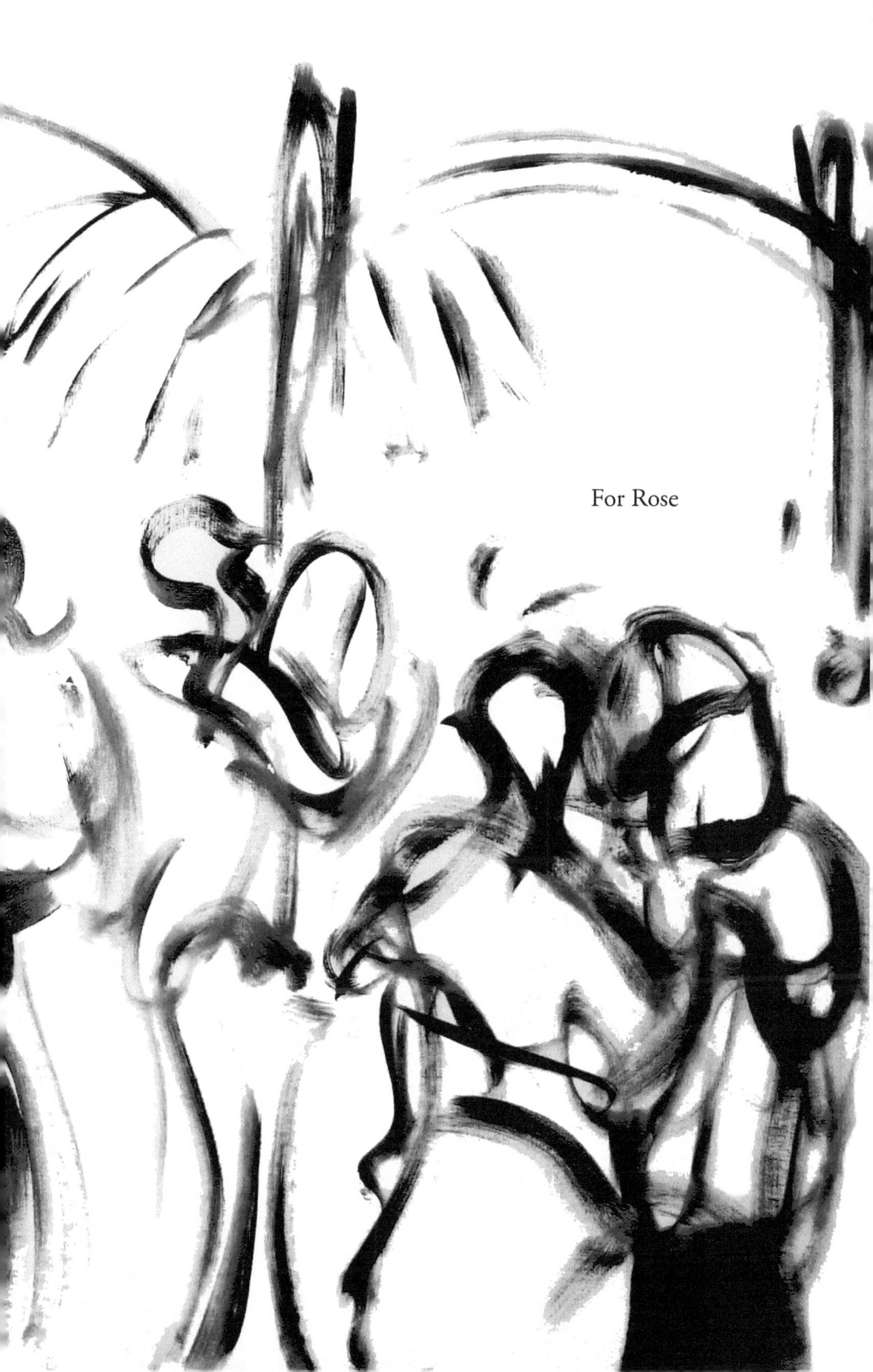

For Rose

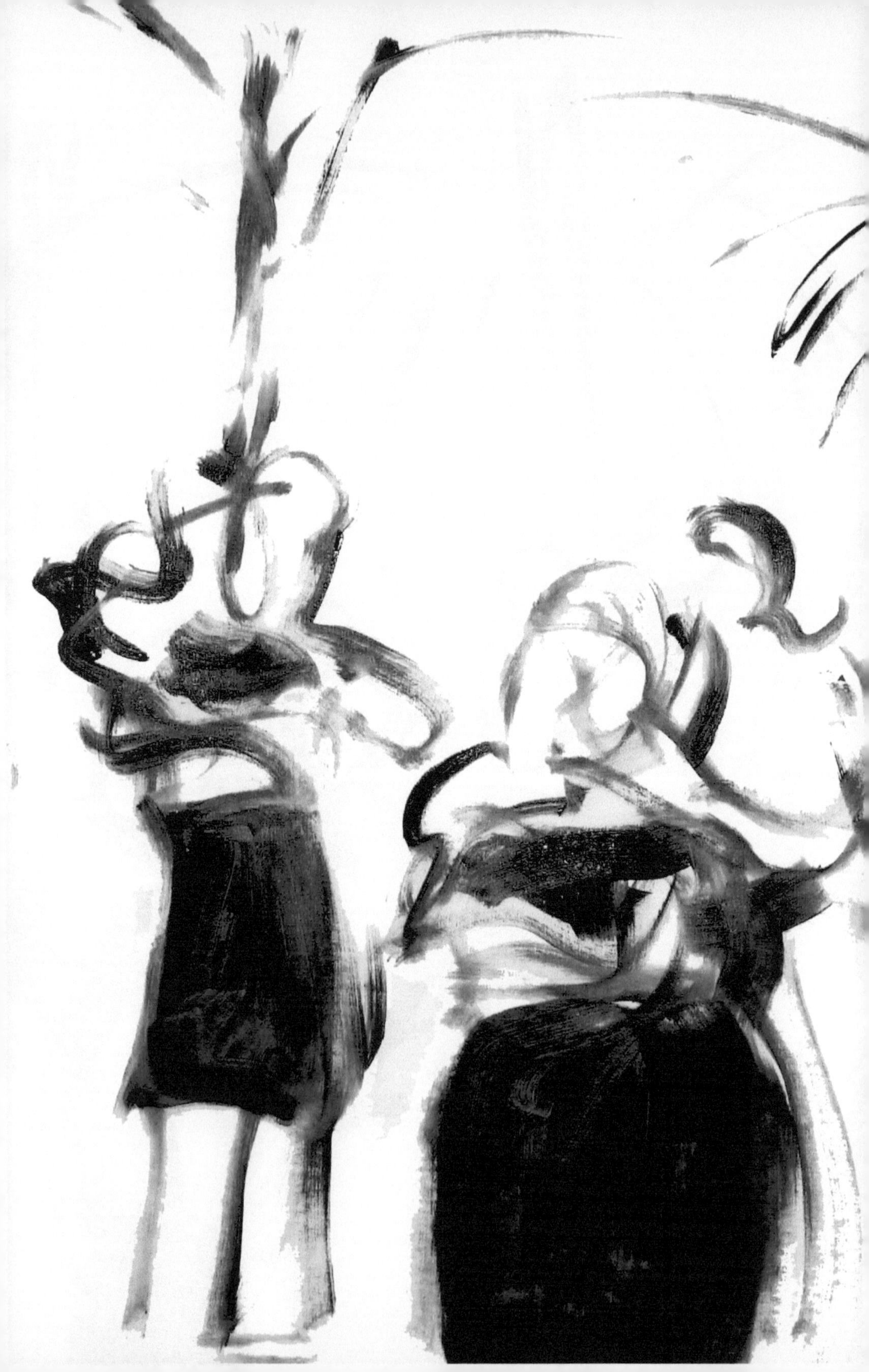

Preface

In my paintings and drawings of people dancing tango, I try to capture the flow of this most sensual dance and the lyrical movements that form its vocabulary. The gesture of a certain step, a certain feeling, a certain note of nostalgia, longing, and . . . love. When couples dance their best, I see shapes of two people dancing as ONE, in these carved moments, conjunctions of time and space. No two moments are ever the same. The constant factor is change, mutability of form in the dim light of the dance floor. In these paintings and drawings, I hope you see the soul of the tango, shifting like sand, or the sea tides that come and come.

It has taken me the years of my life to attain simplicity. Here you see an instant of those years. My technique has evolved from many years of doing figure drawings of people and nudes. During six years in Tokyo, I noticed all around me Japanese calligraphy, admired writing and characters beautifully drawn. I drank deeply from this fountain of aesthetics and line. I understood perhaps only half of the intended meaning, but the quality and presence of the pure line captivated me. The strokes flowed as easily as the dance.

Now that I am based in Buenos Aires, I see more than the fluidity of physical movement in the tango between the dancers. Beyond formal movement, the tango is the complex relationship between two souls, the flow of profound sensuality, and in some cases, a type of violence that only those who live in this macho society would fully comprehend. The dance is a mere technicality.

Two people locked in a sensual embrace, dancing. Bodies intertwined. Flowing, on paper, forever.

—Mộng-Lan

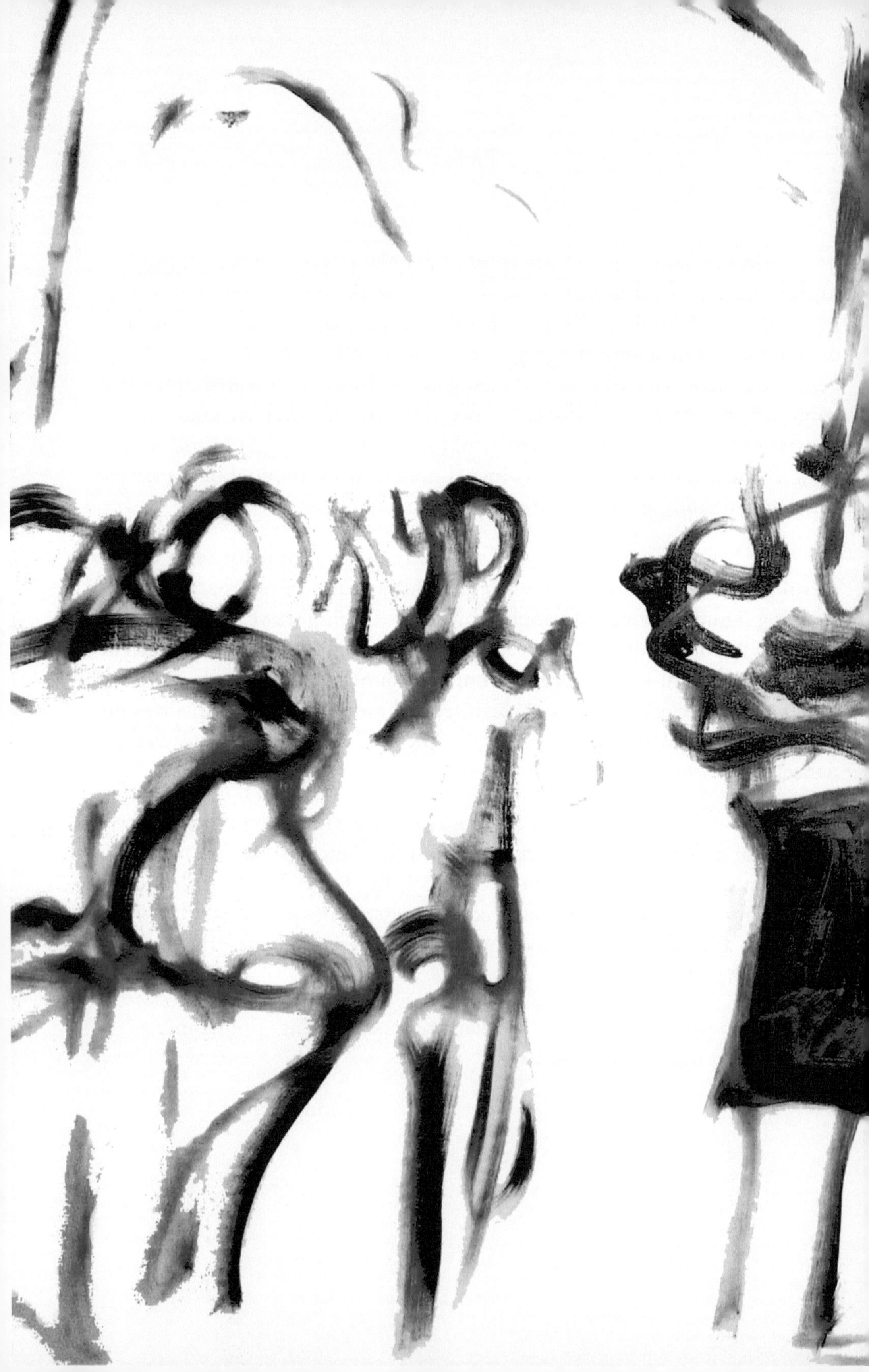

Esperándote

Waiting for you

"… y el corazon me suplicó
que te buscara y que le diera tu querer"
—José María Contursi

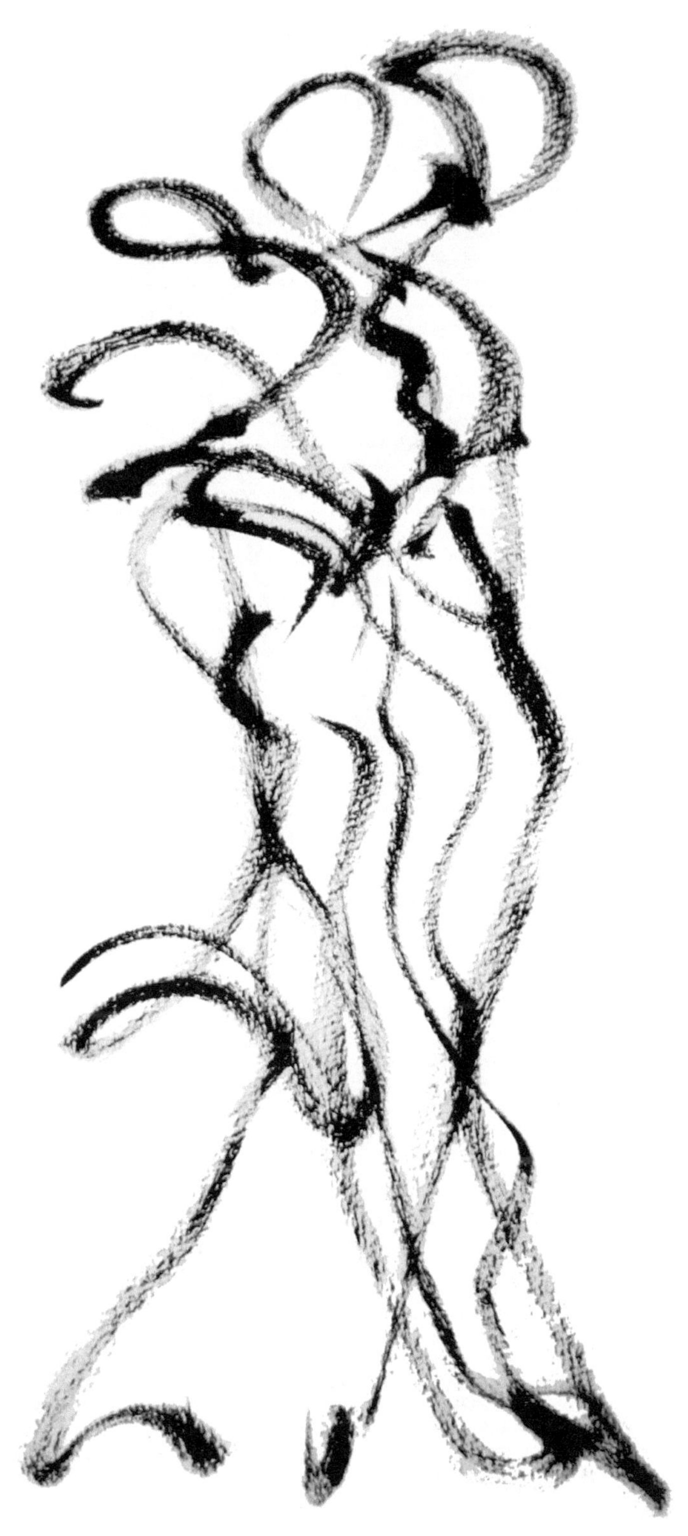

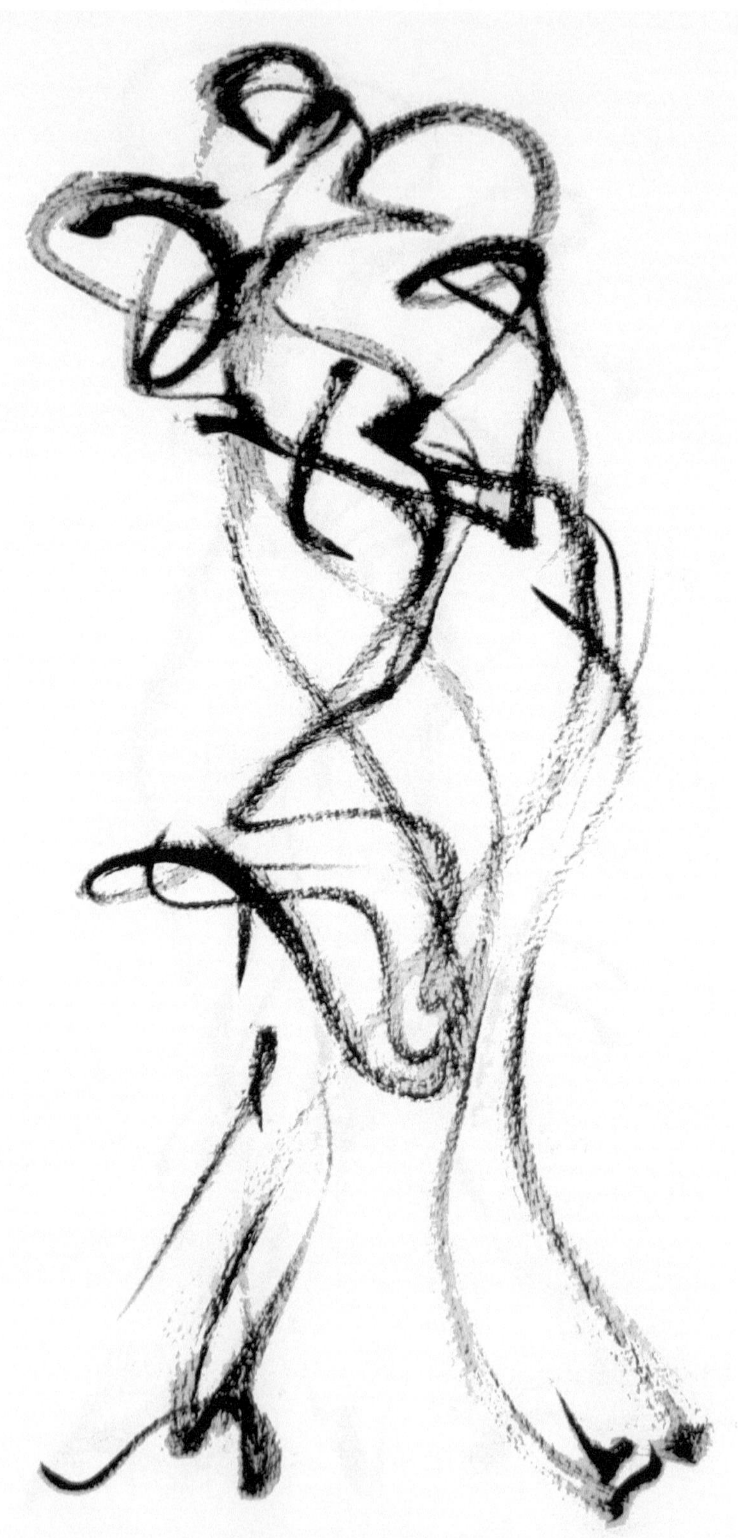

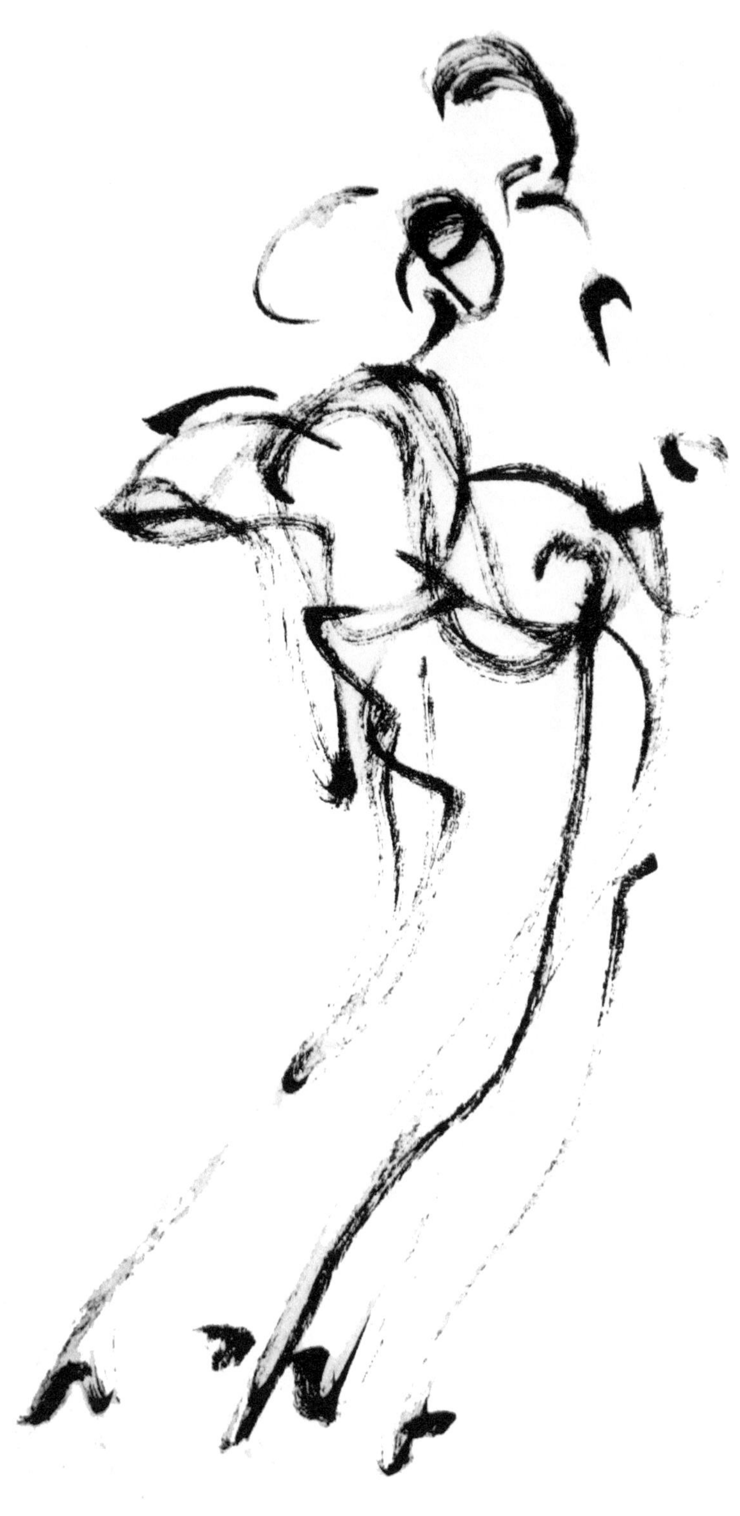

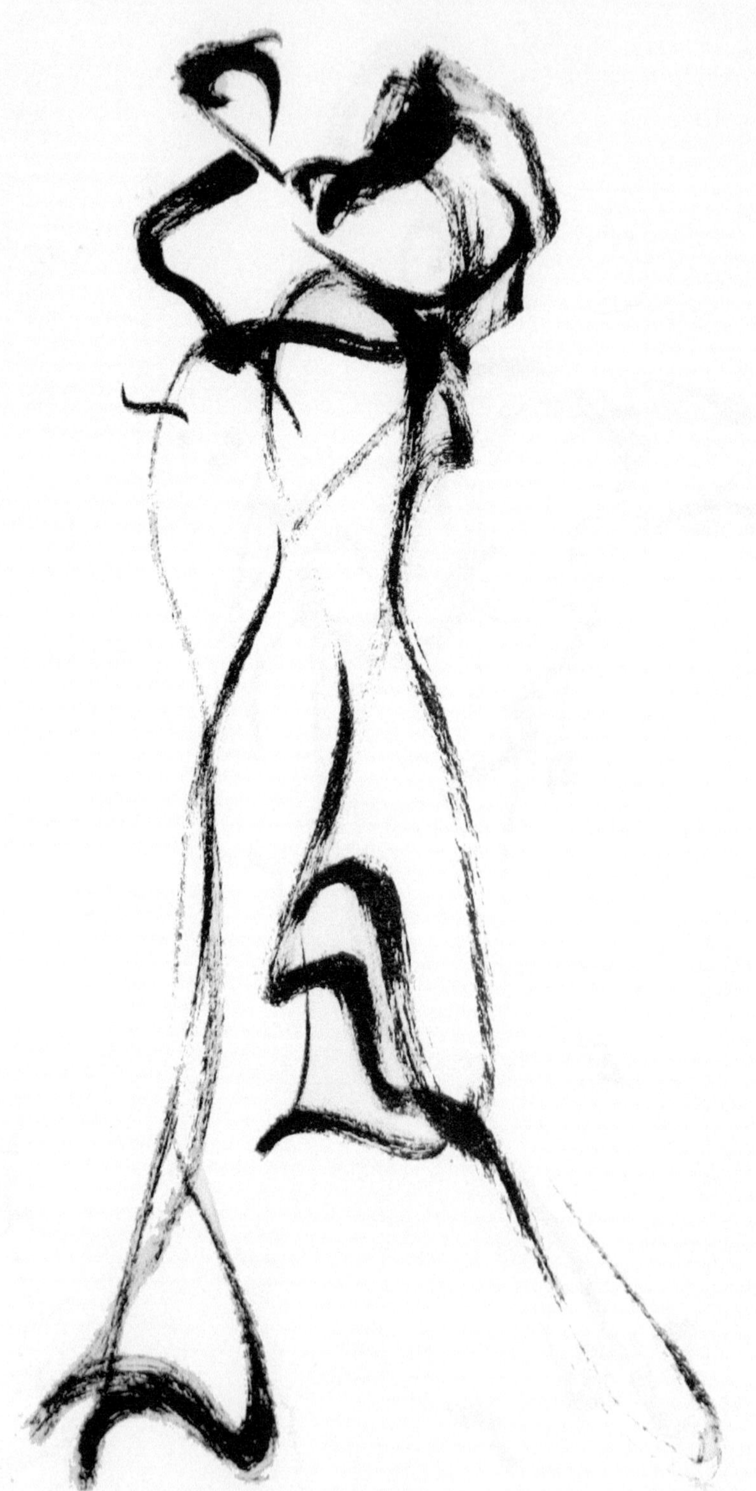

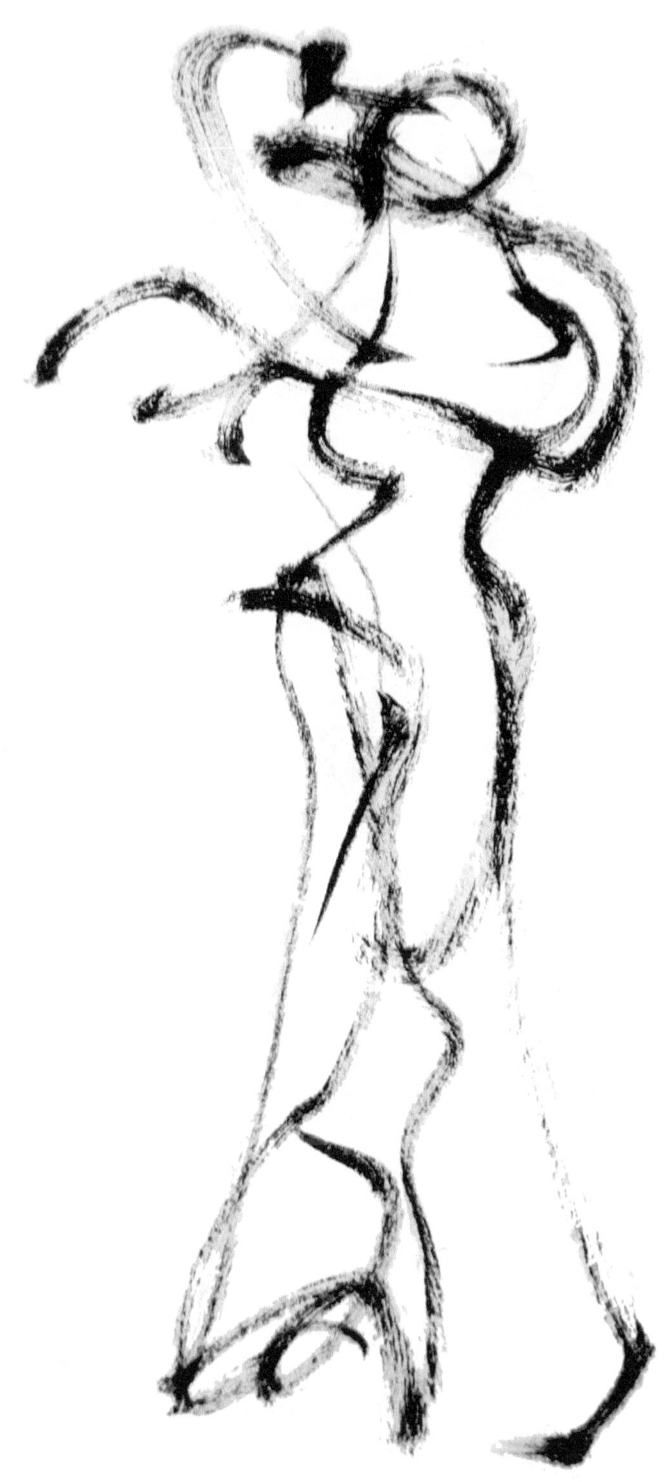

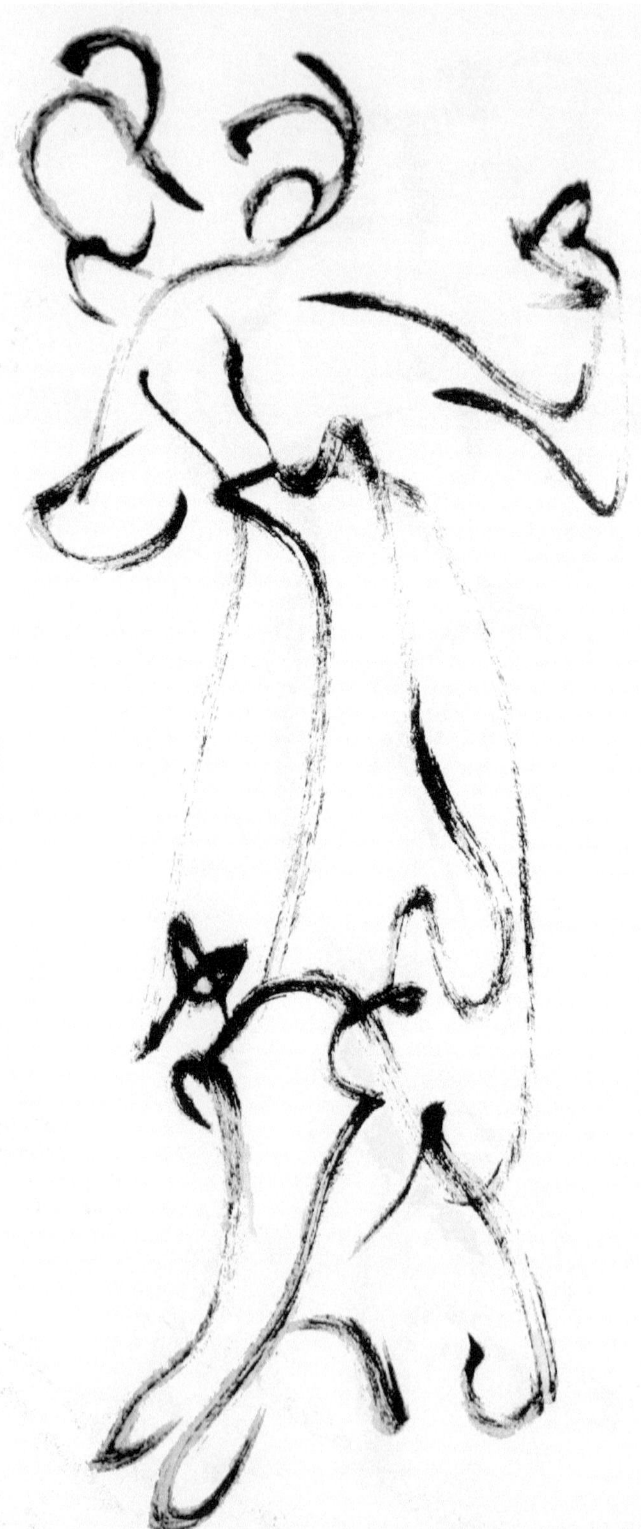
Mộng Lan 2003

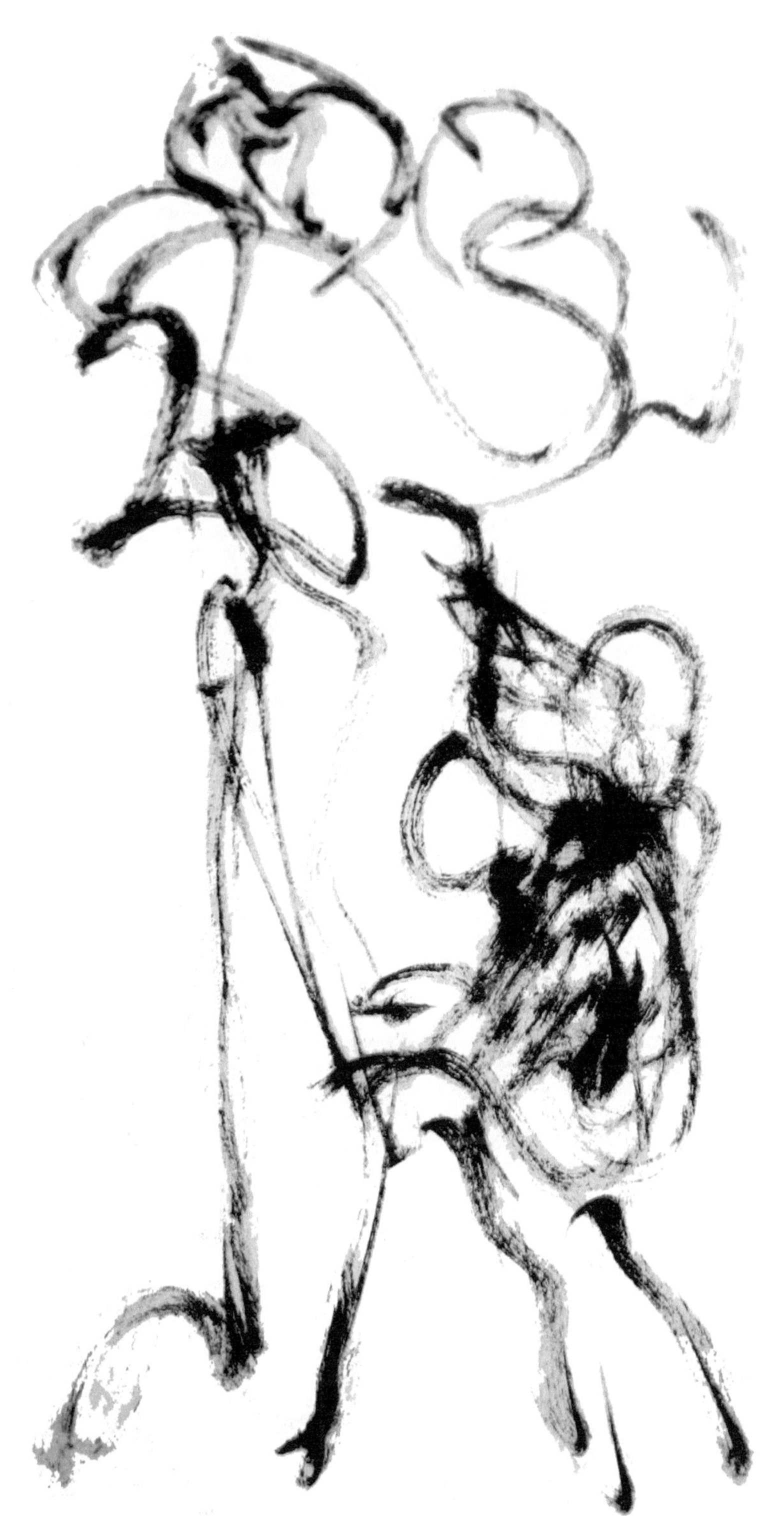

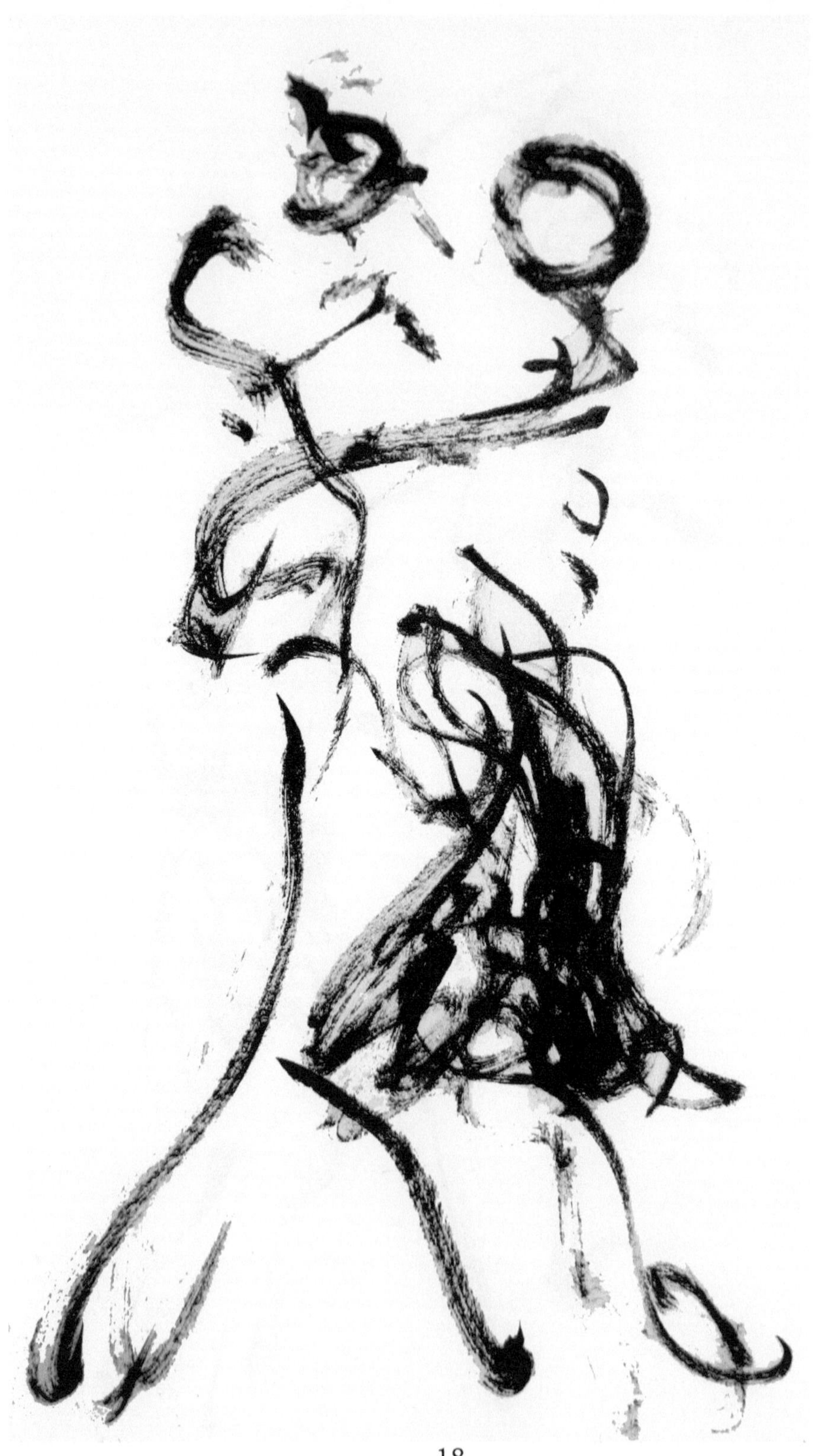

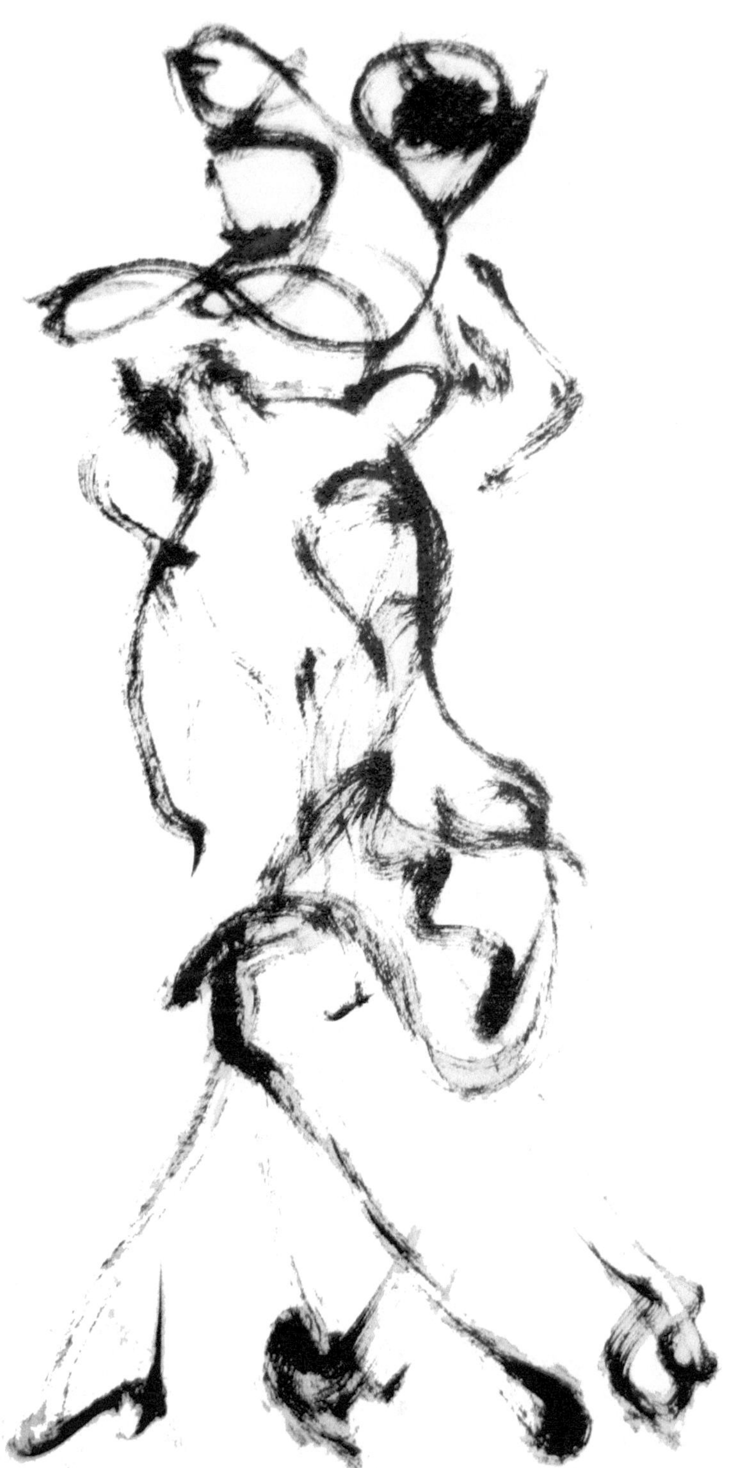

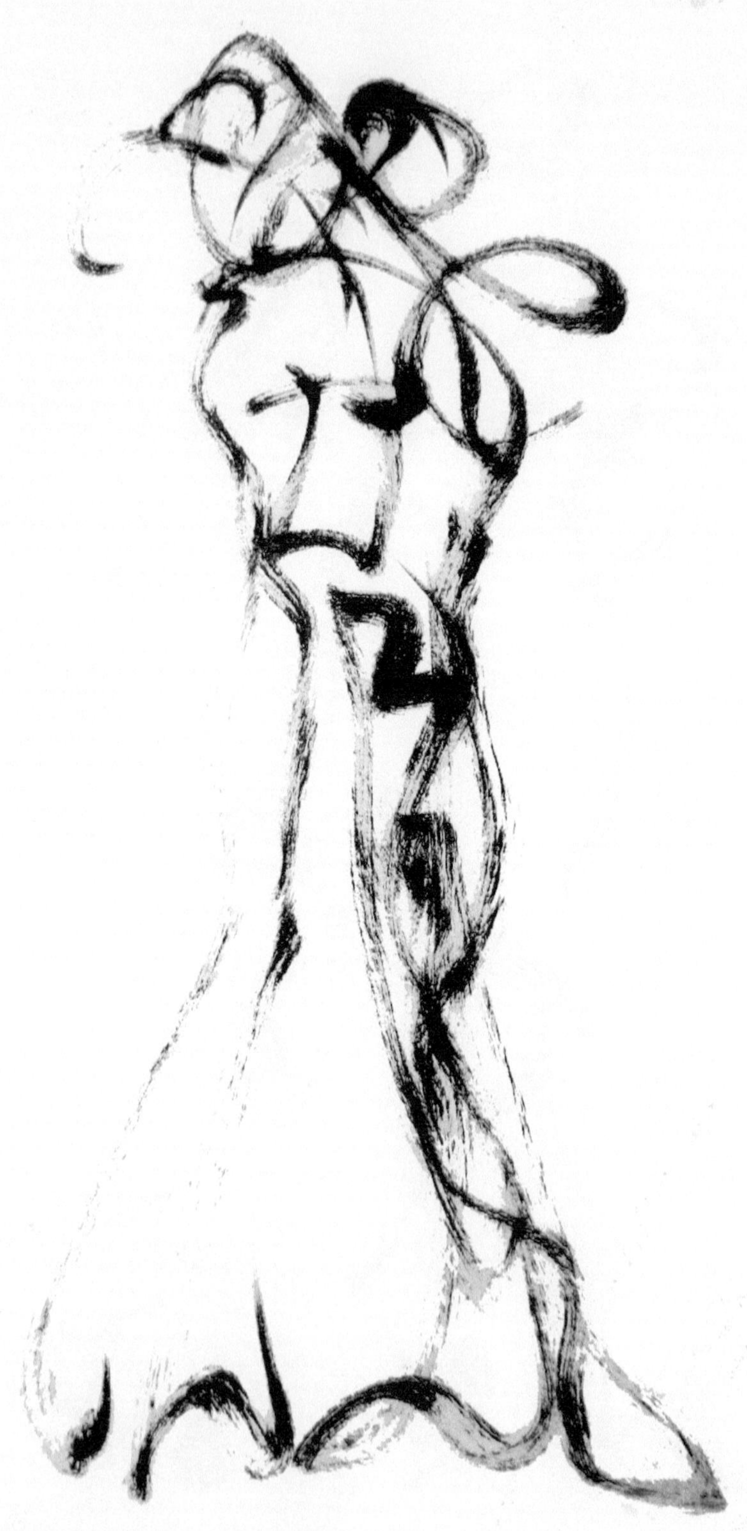
Ming Lan 2008

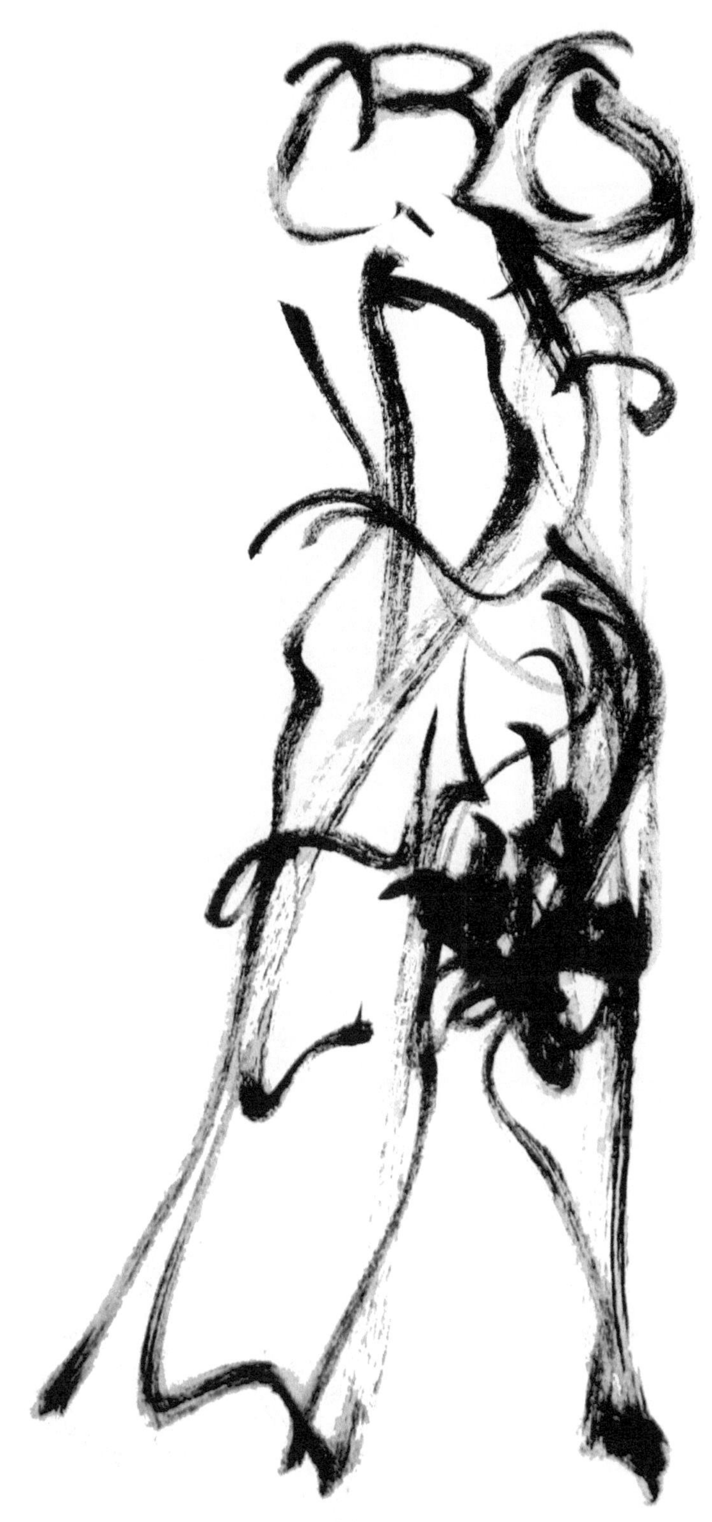

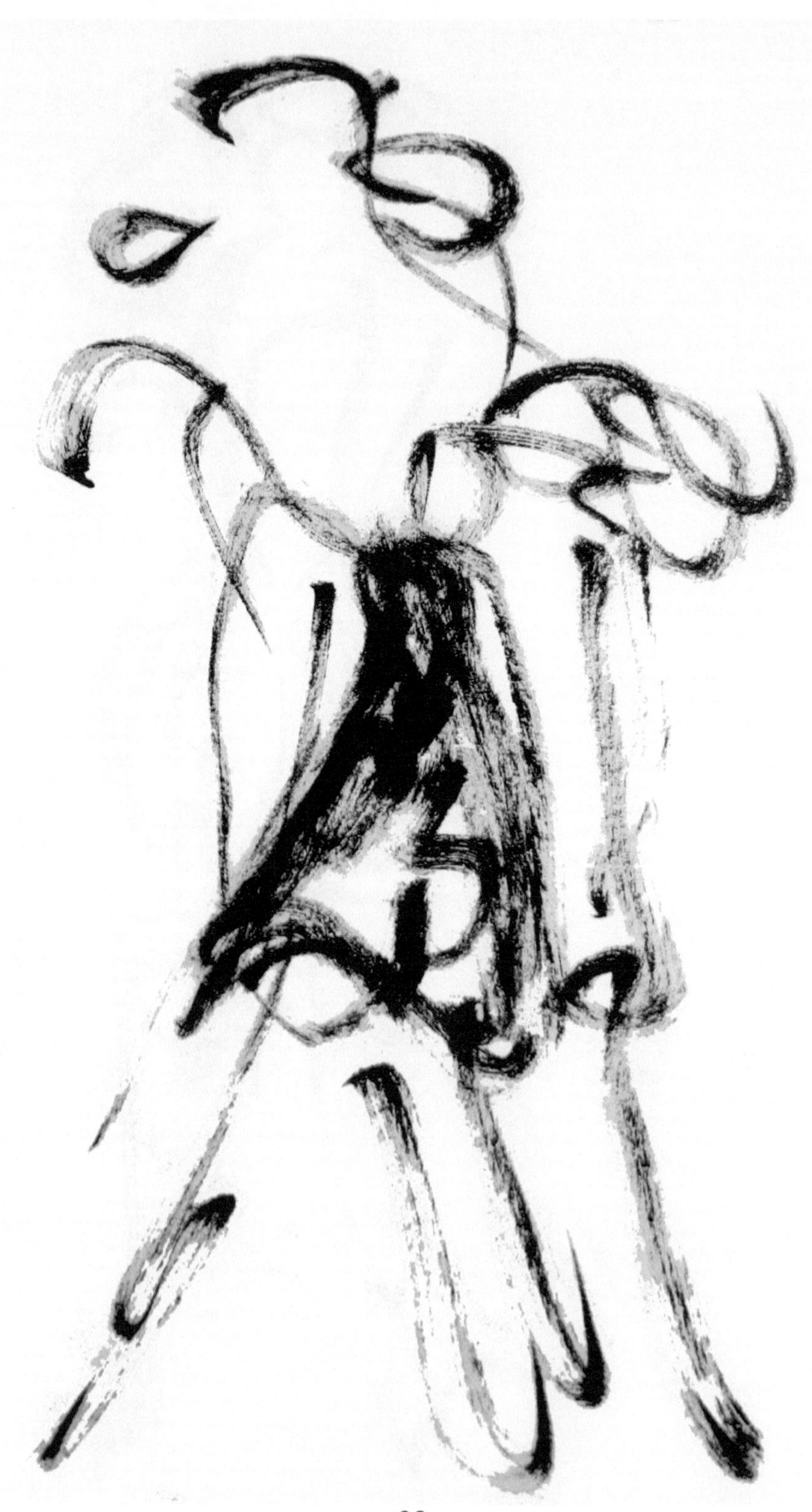

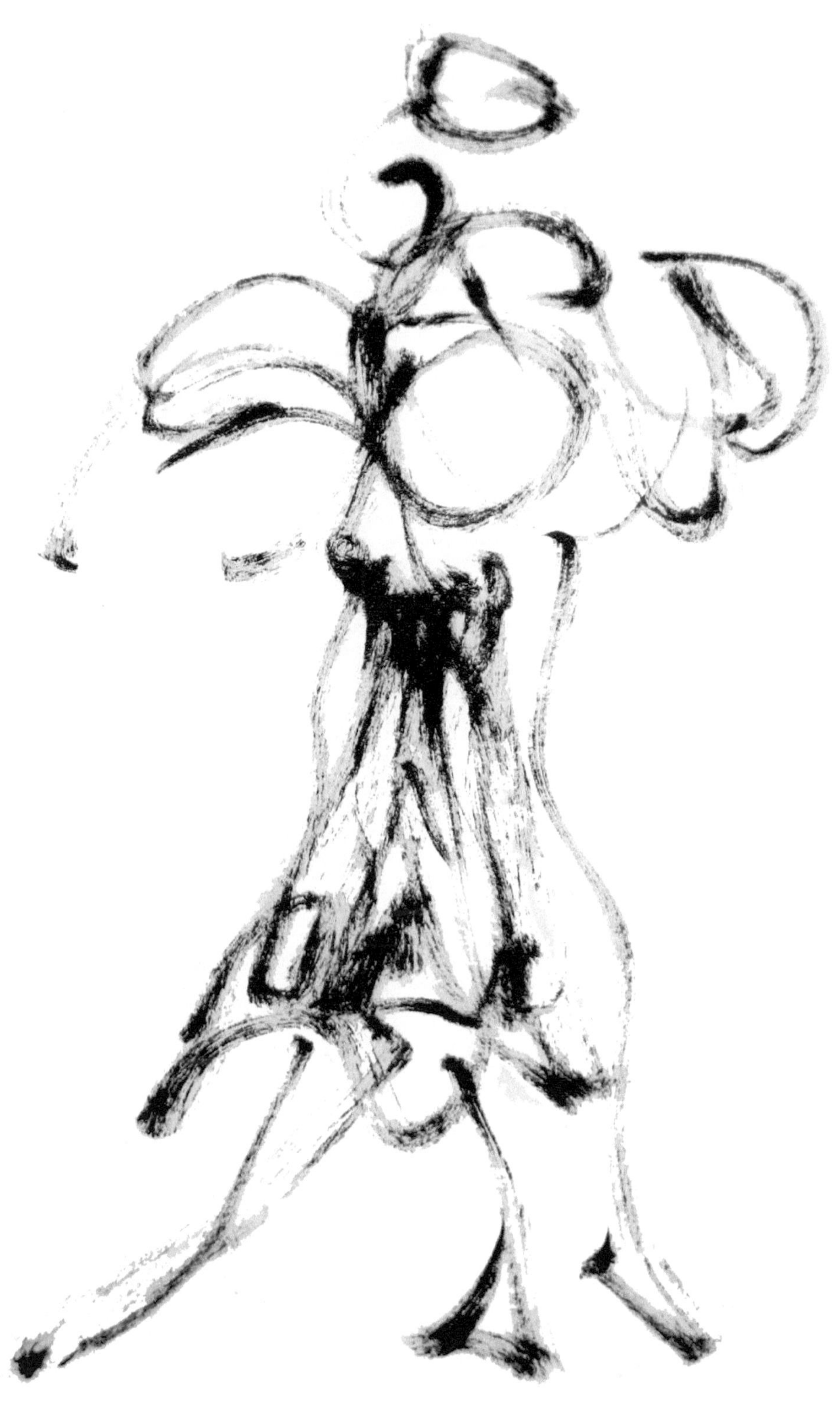

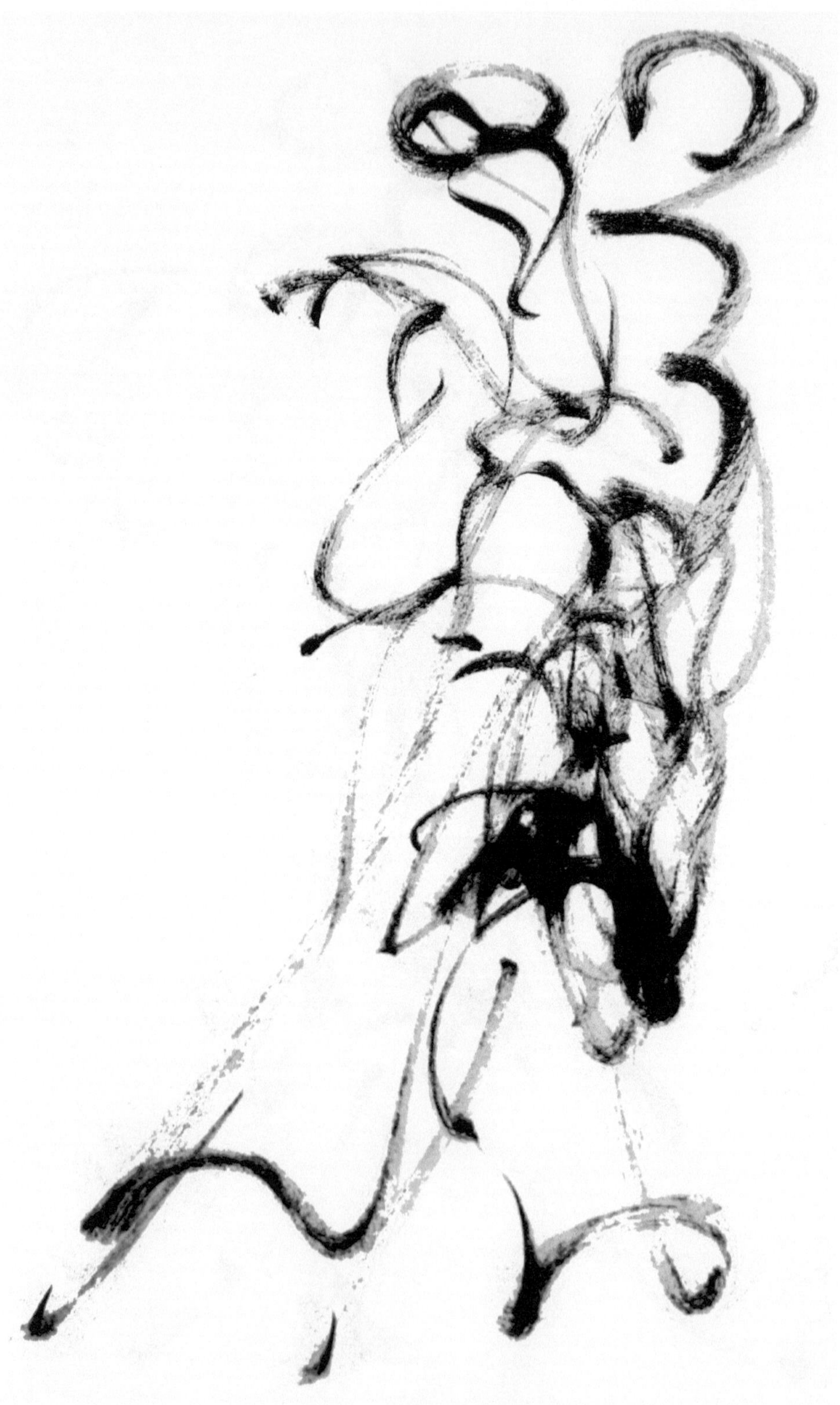

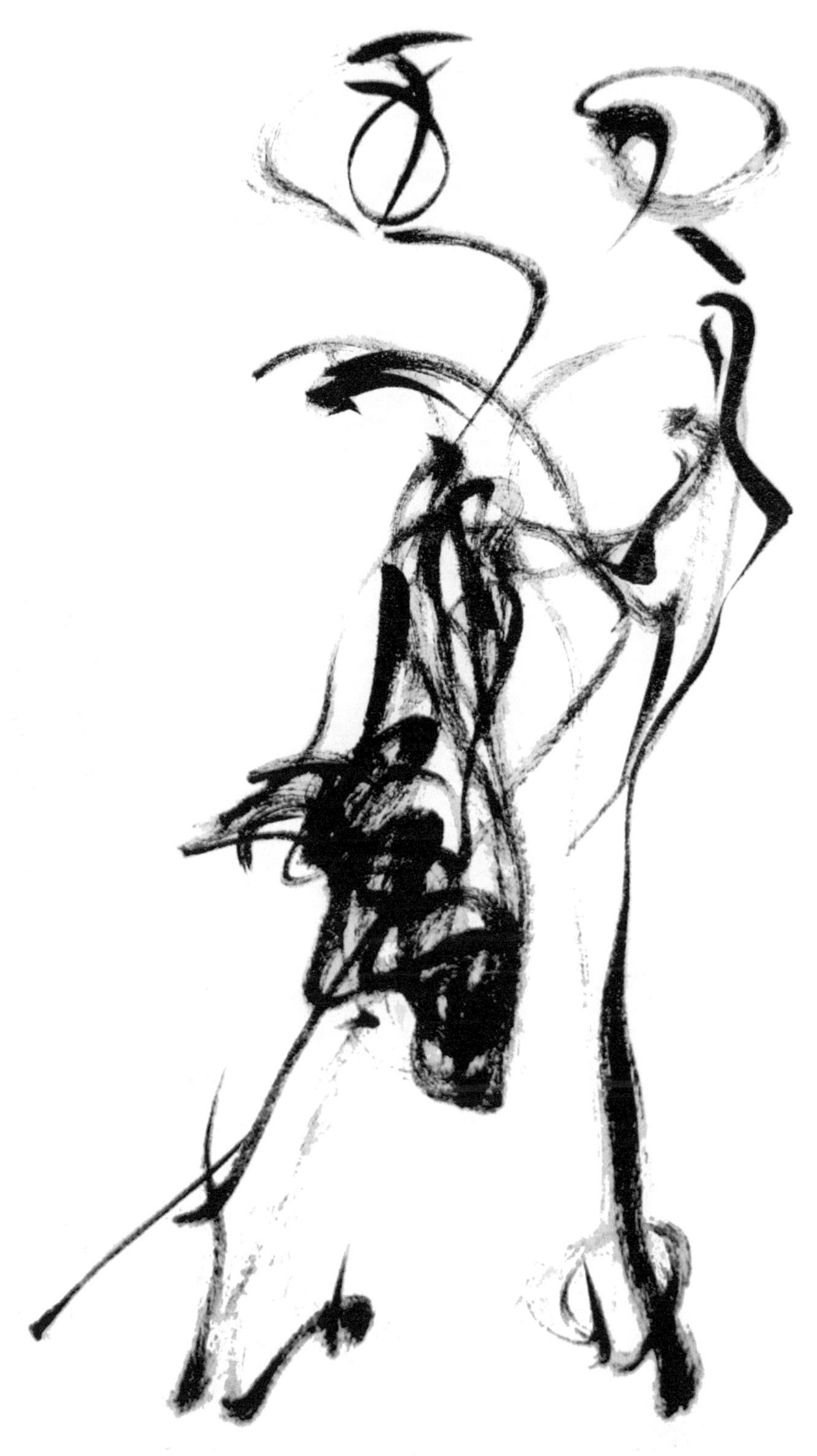

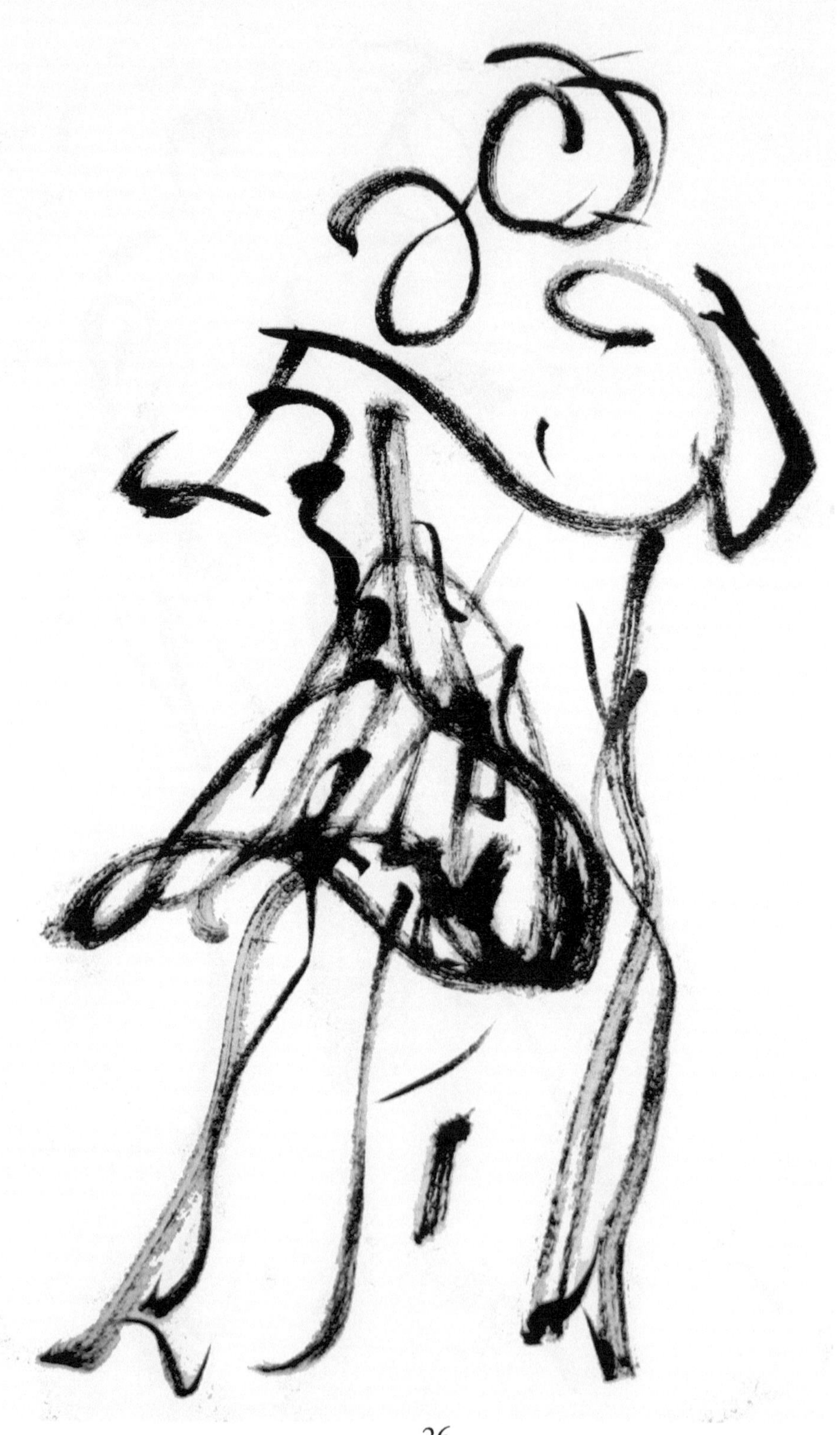

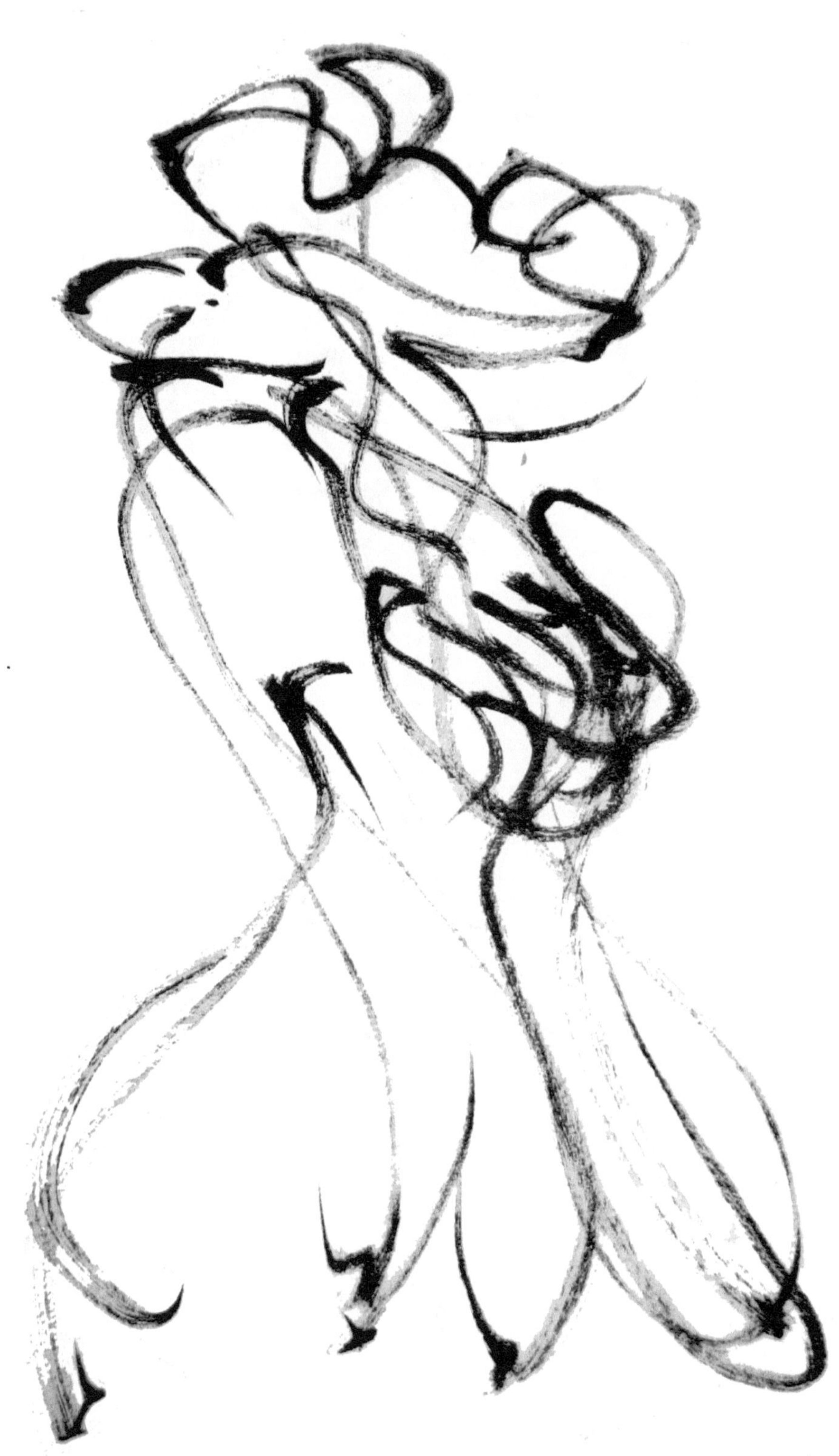

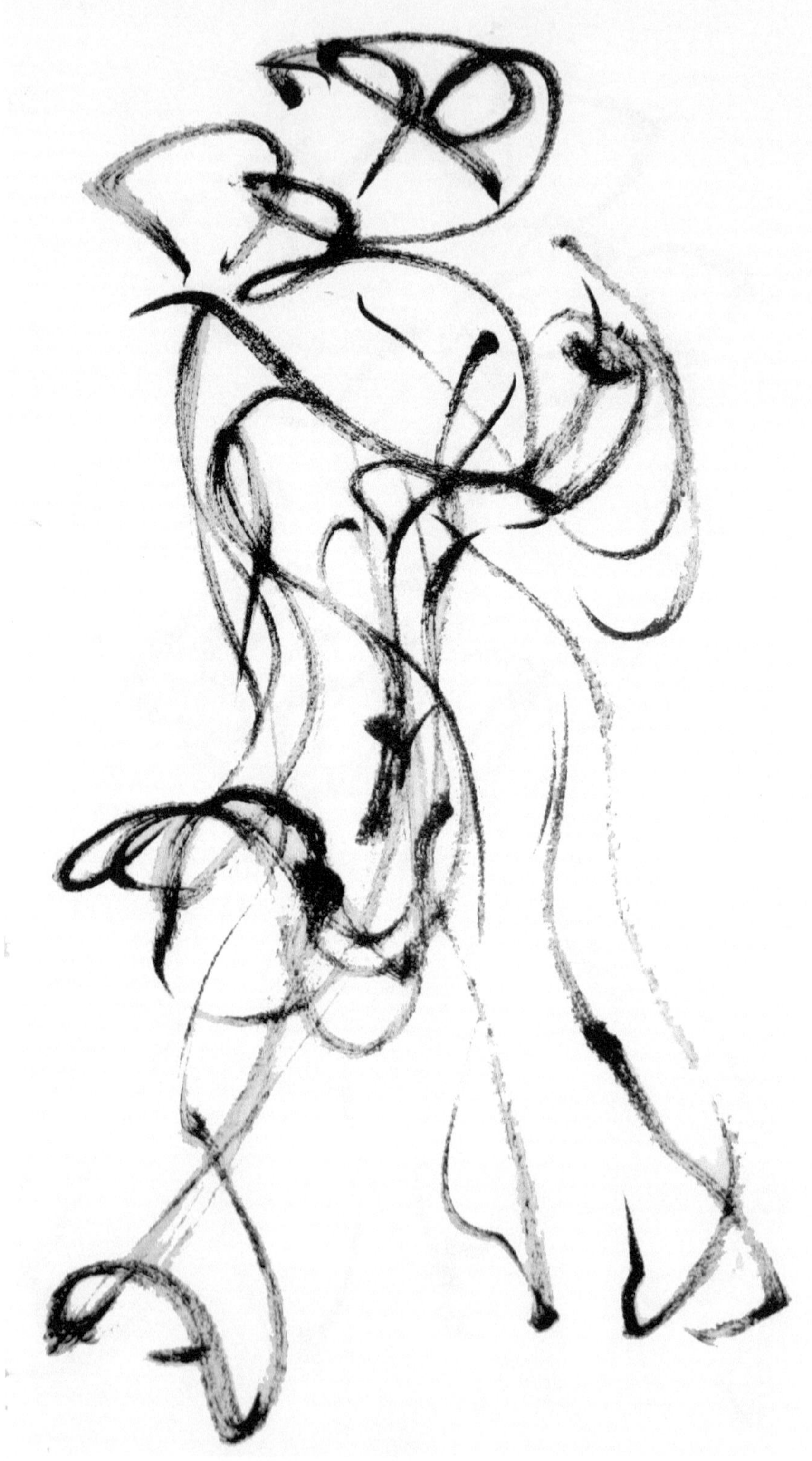

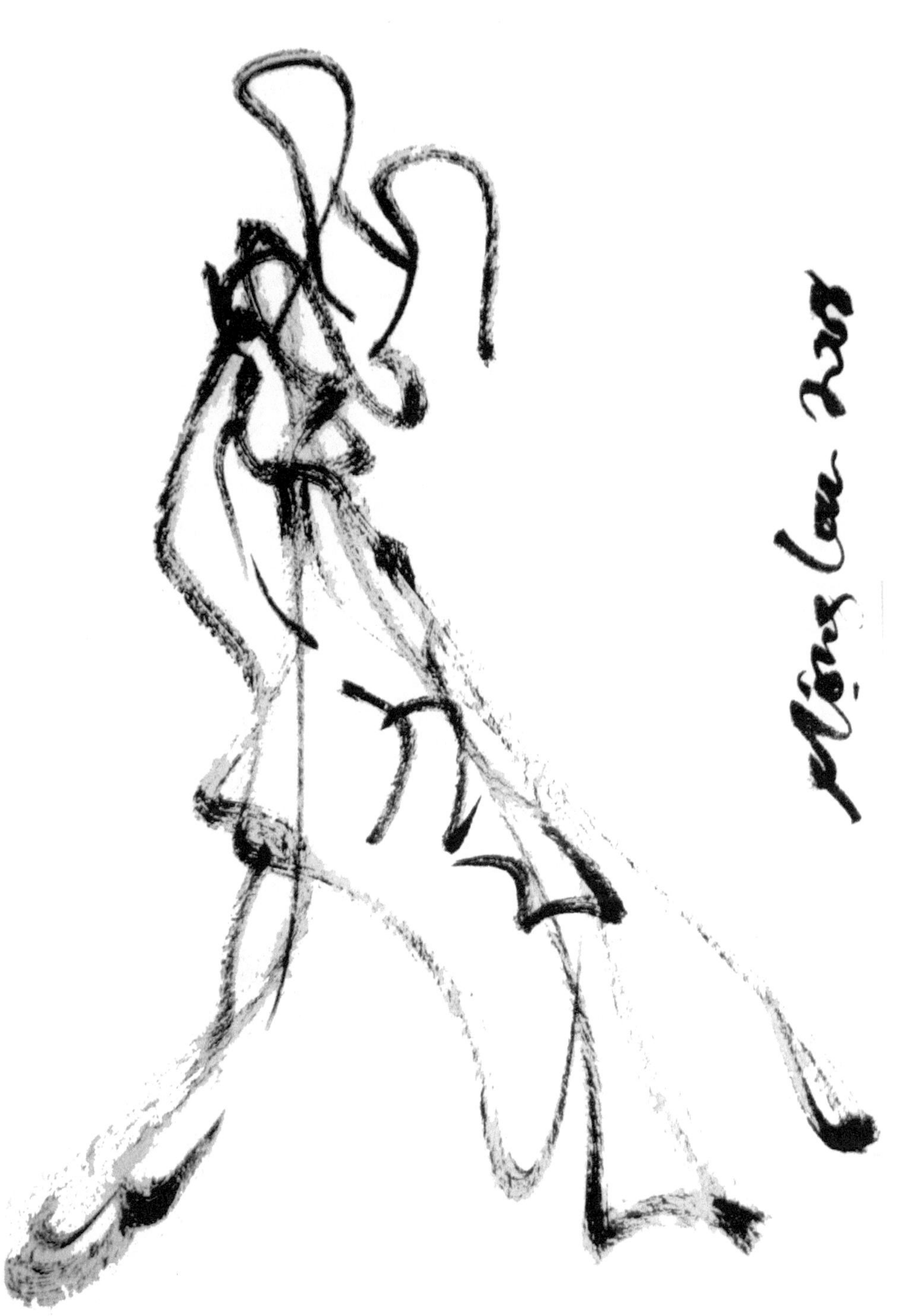

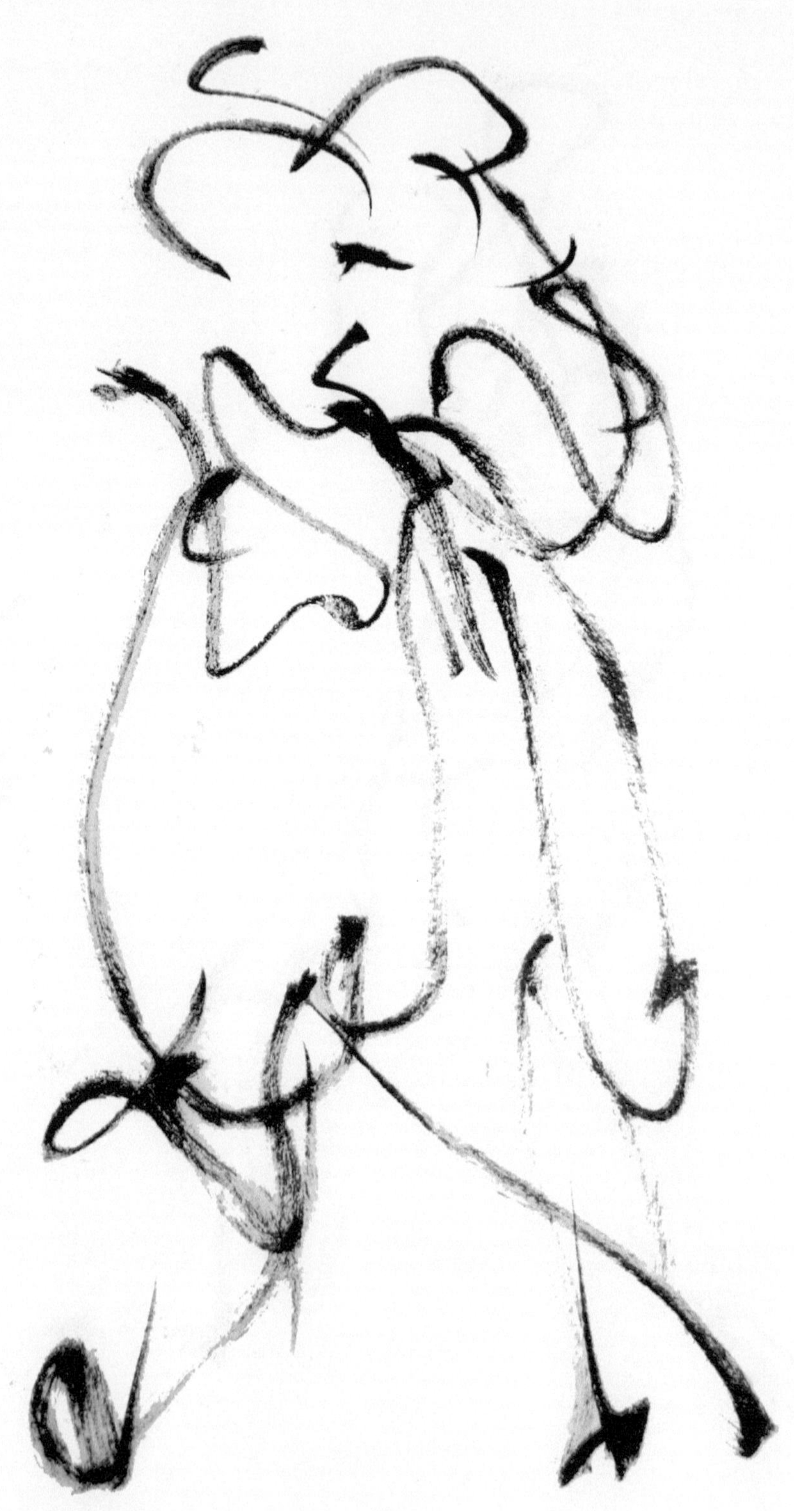

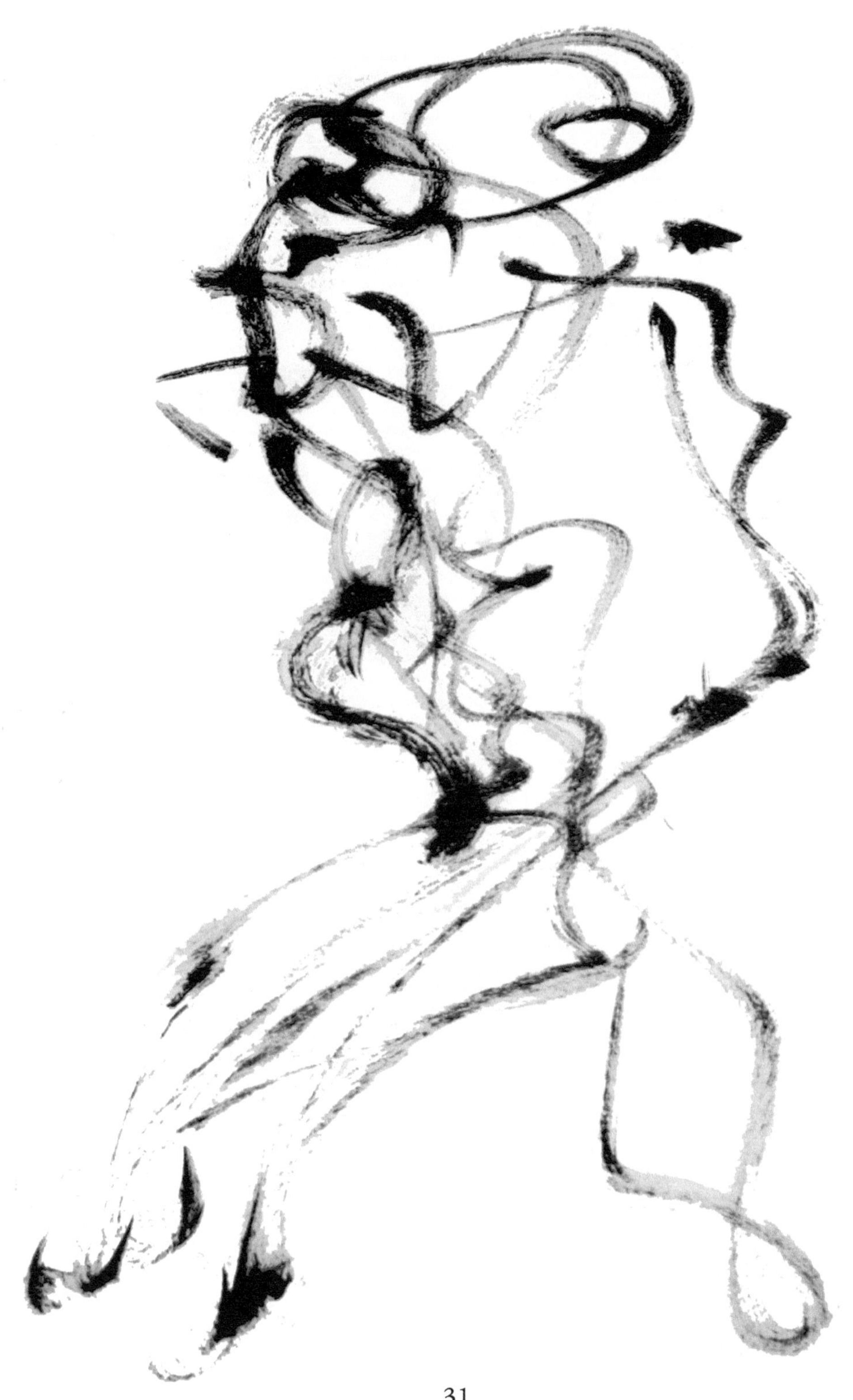

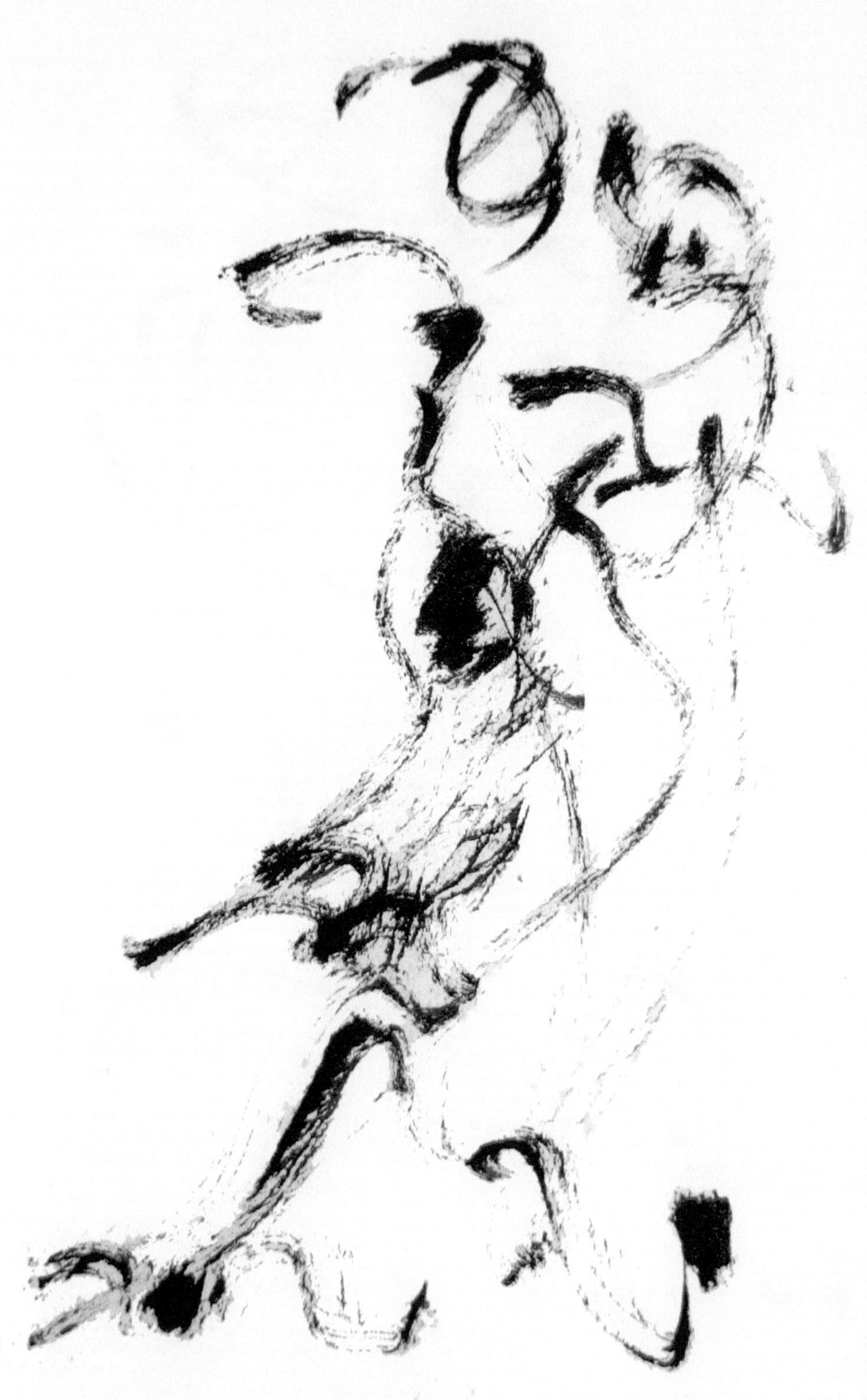

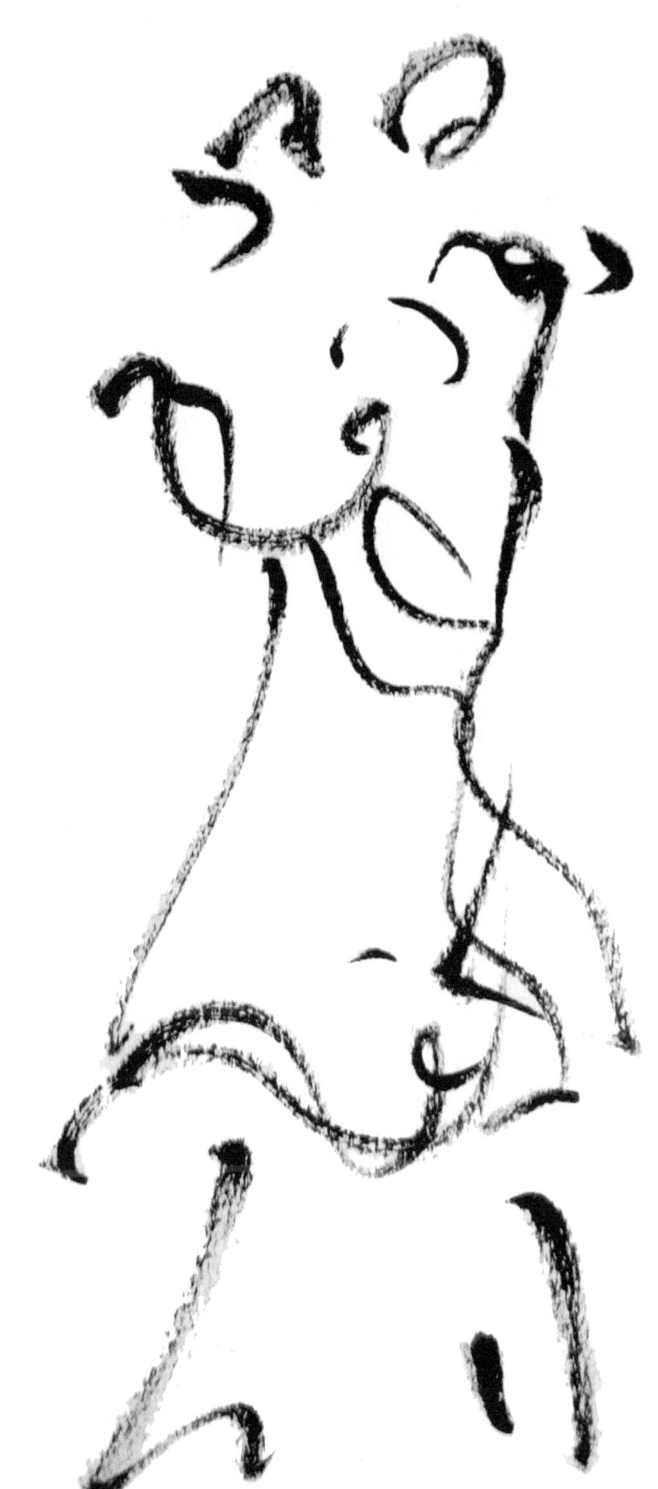

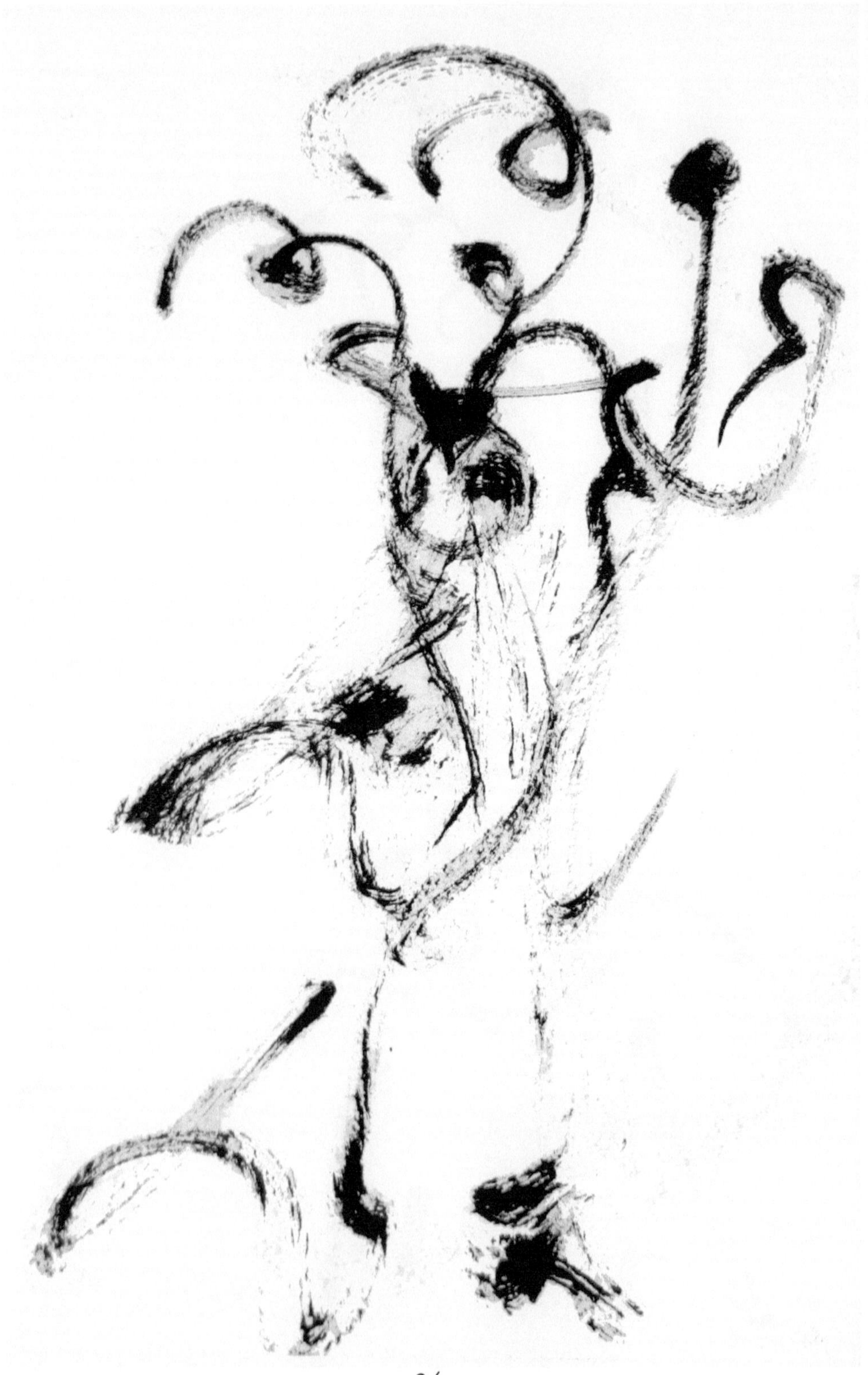

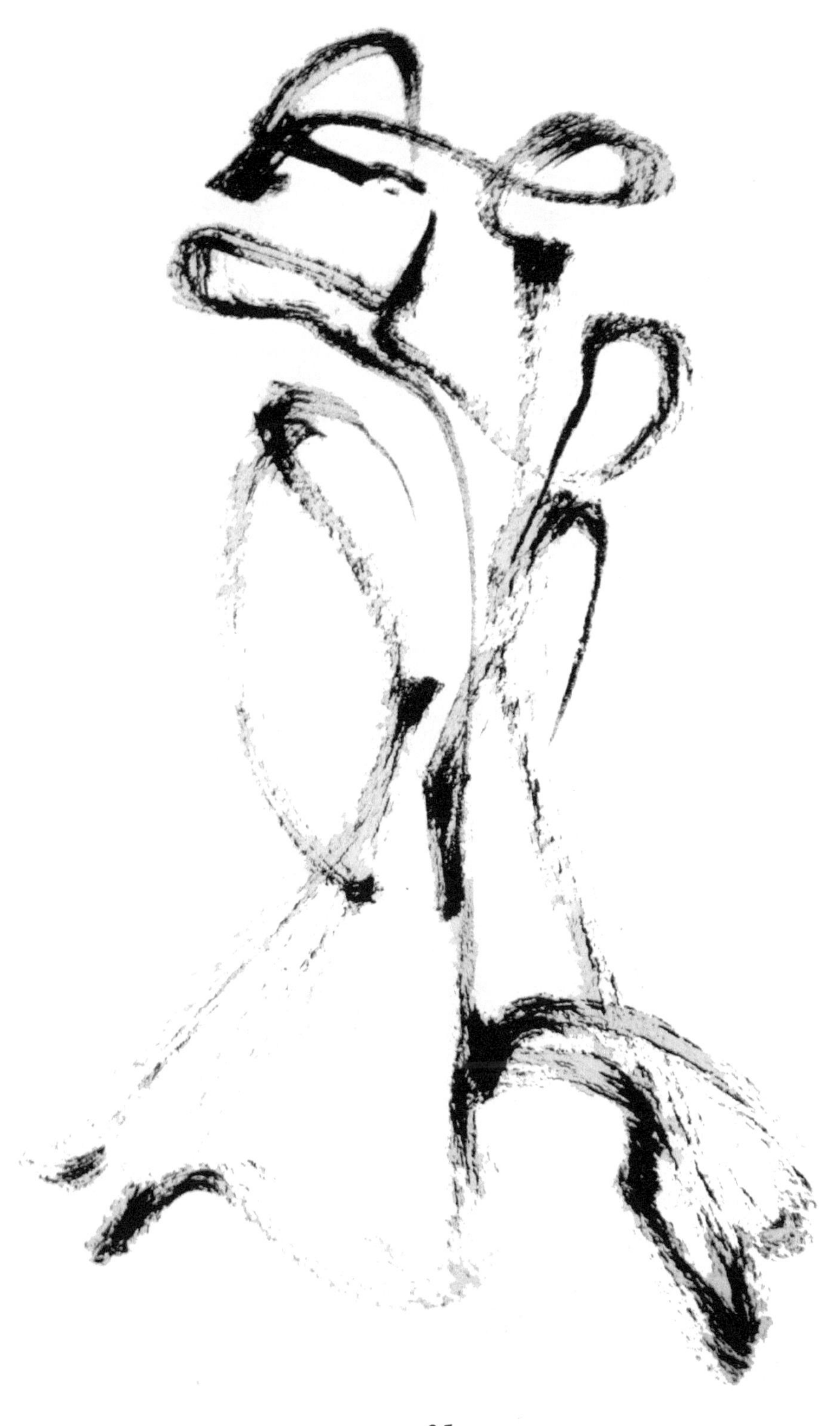

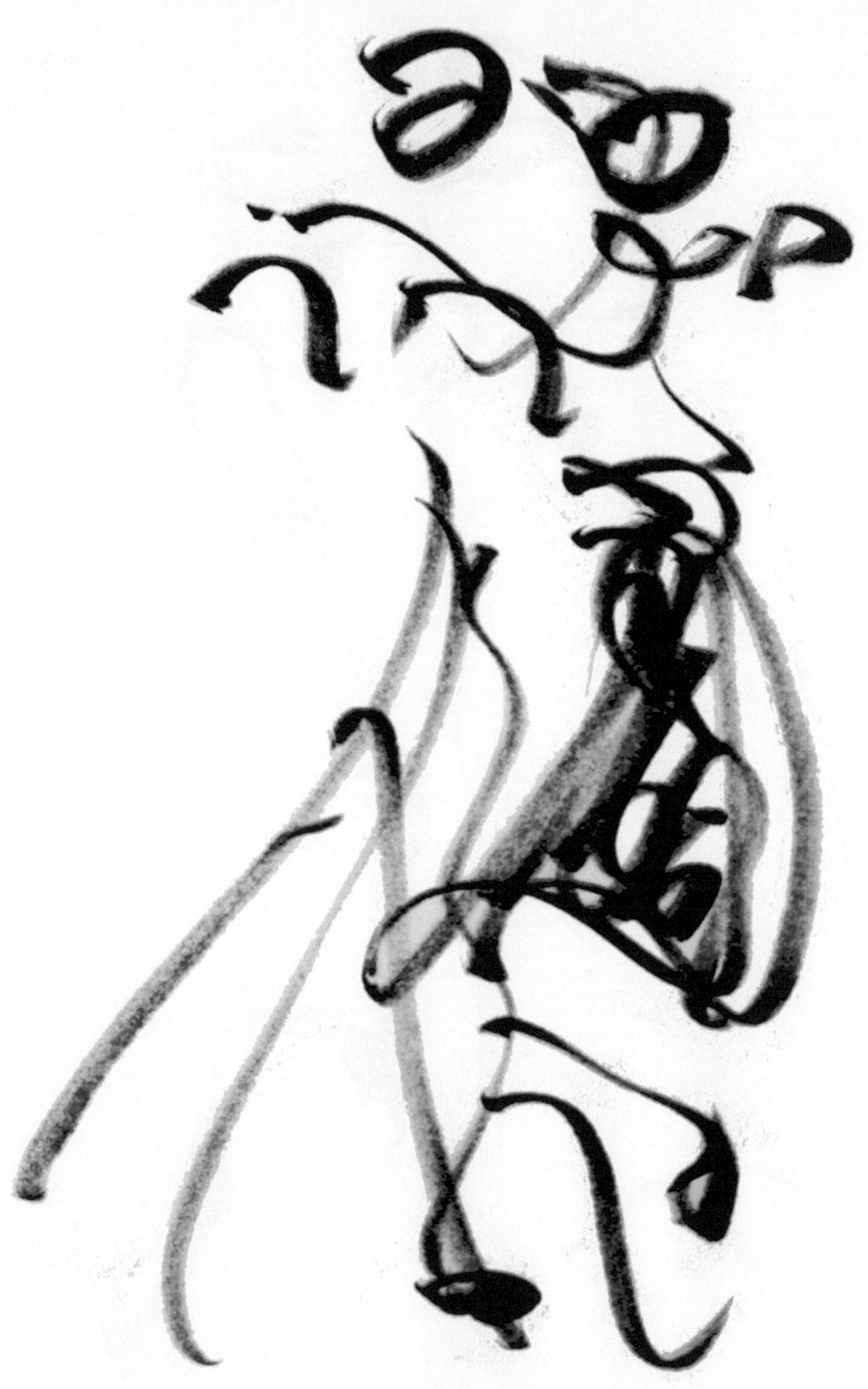

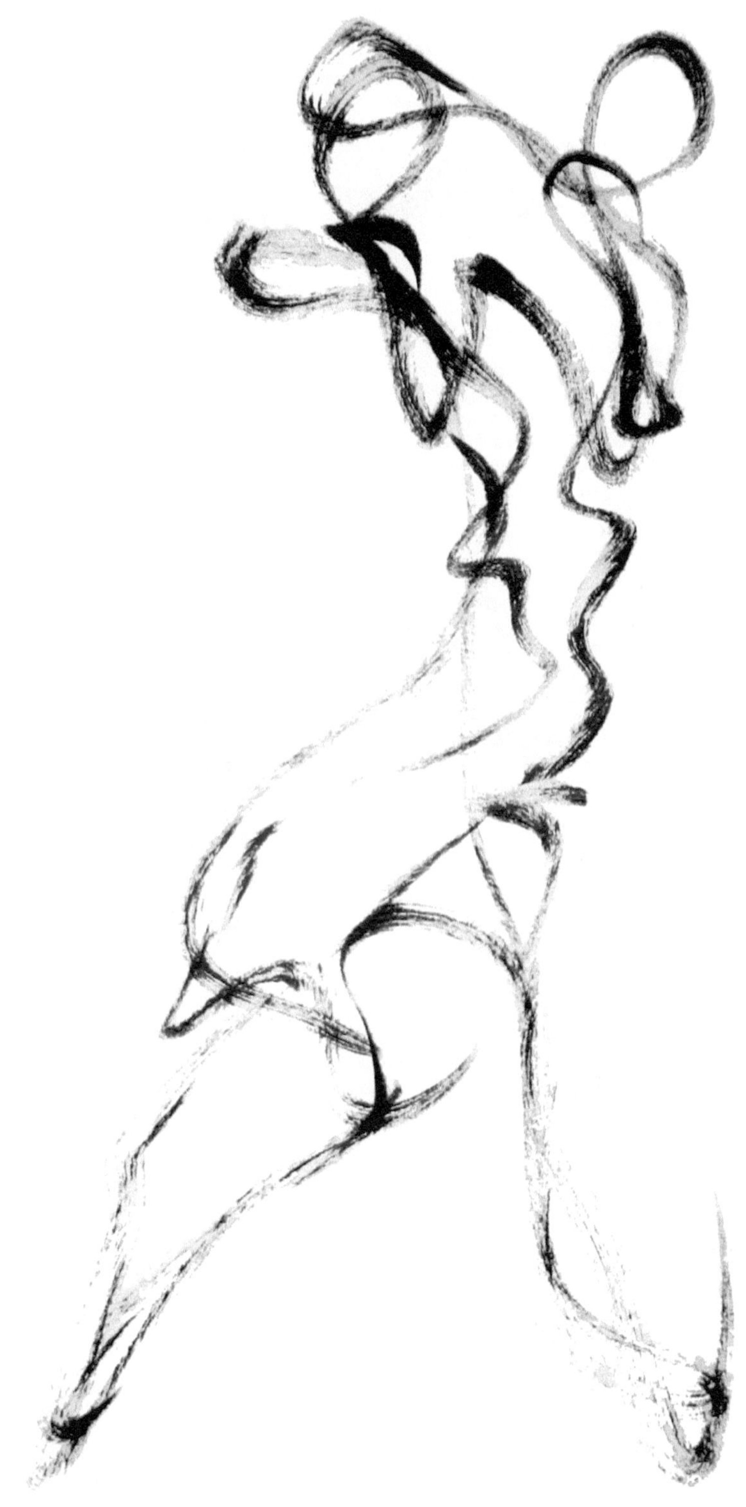

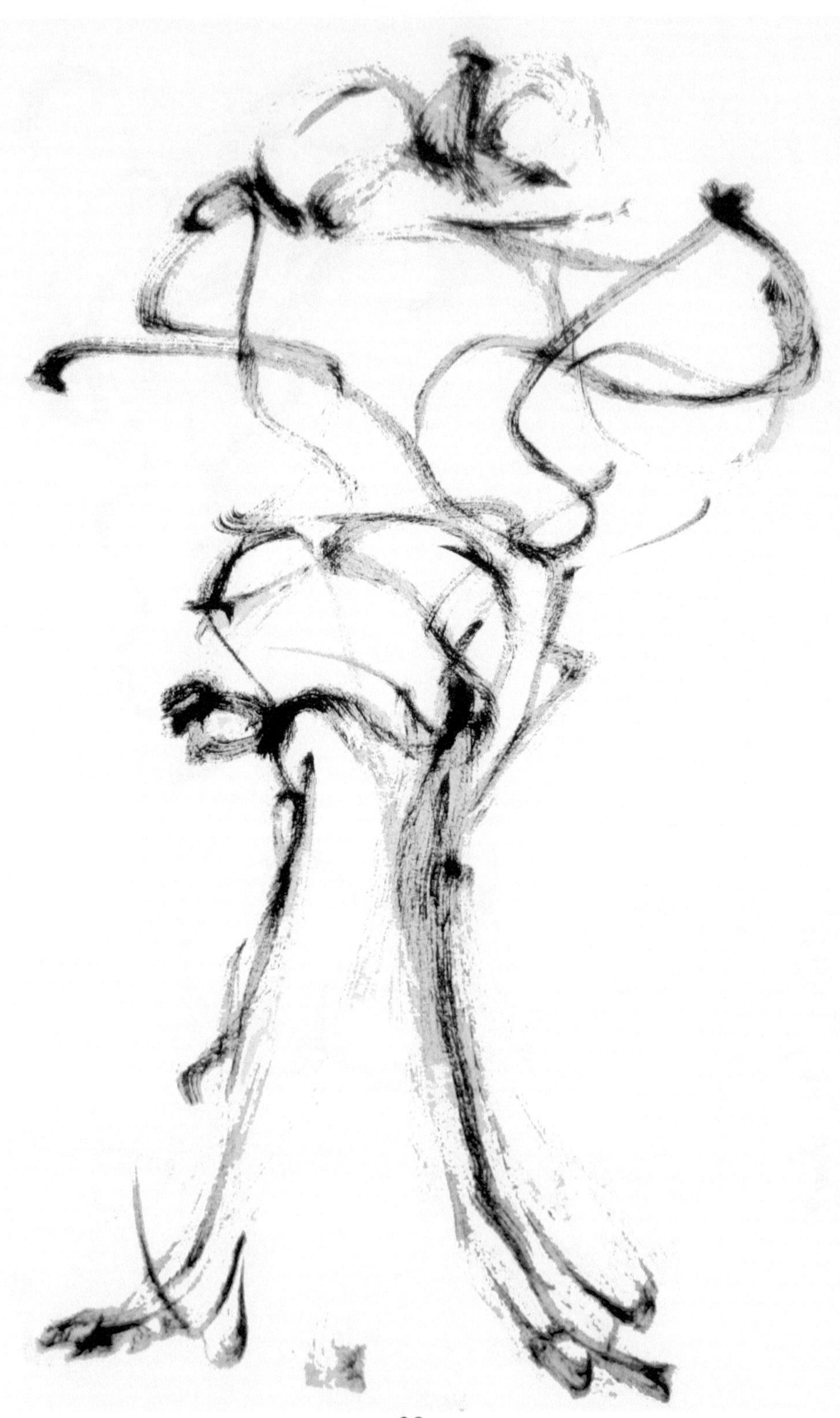

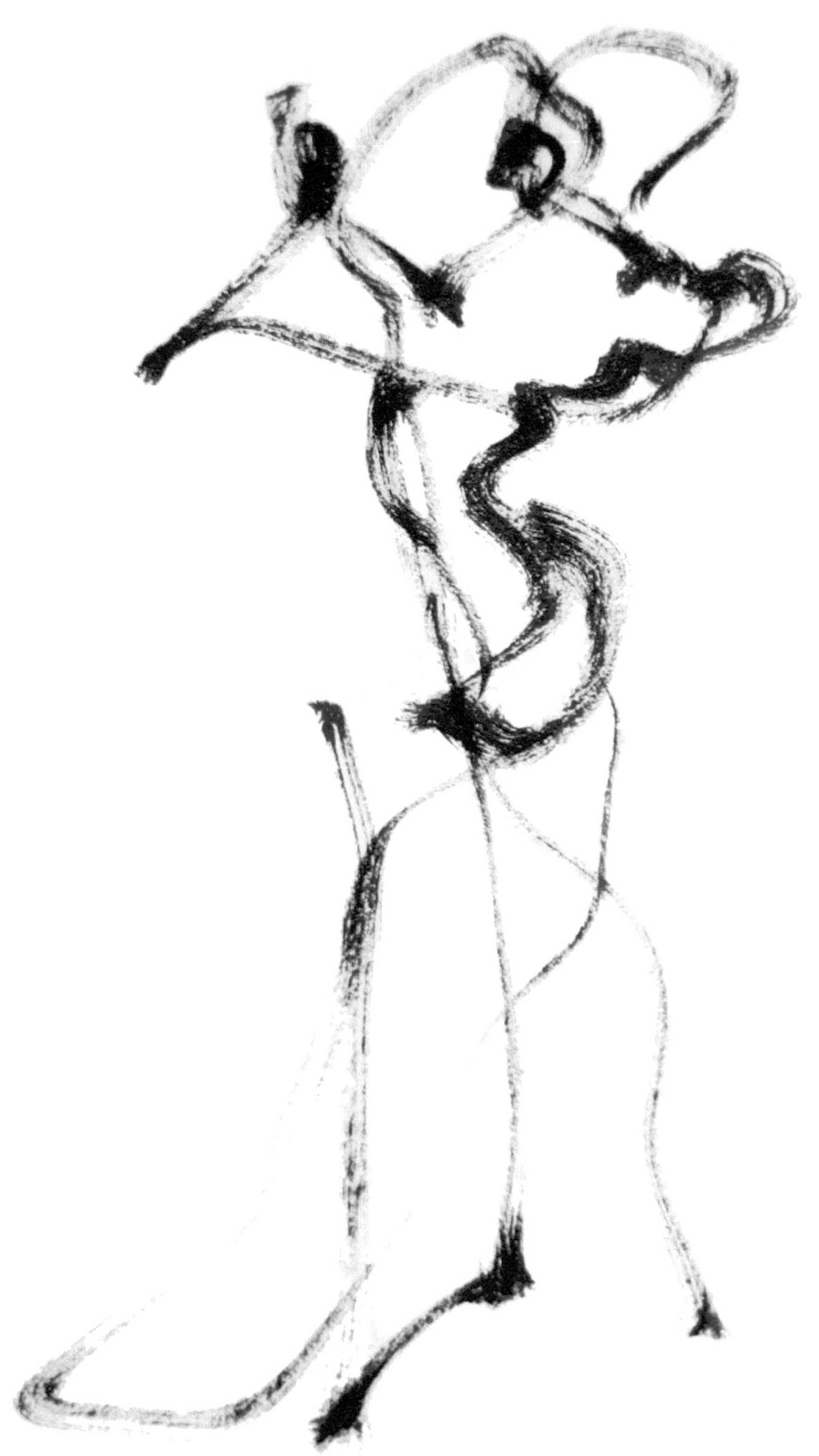

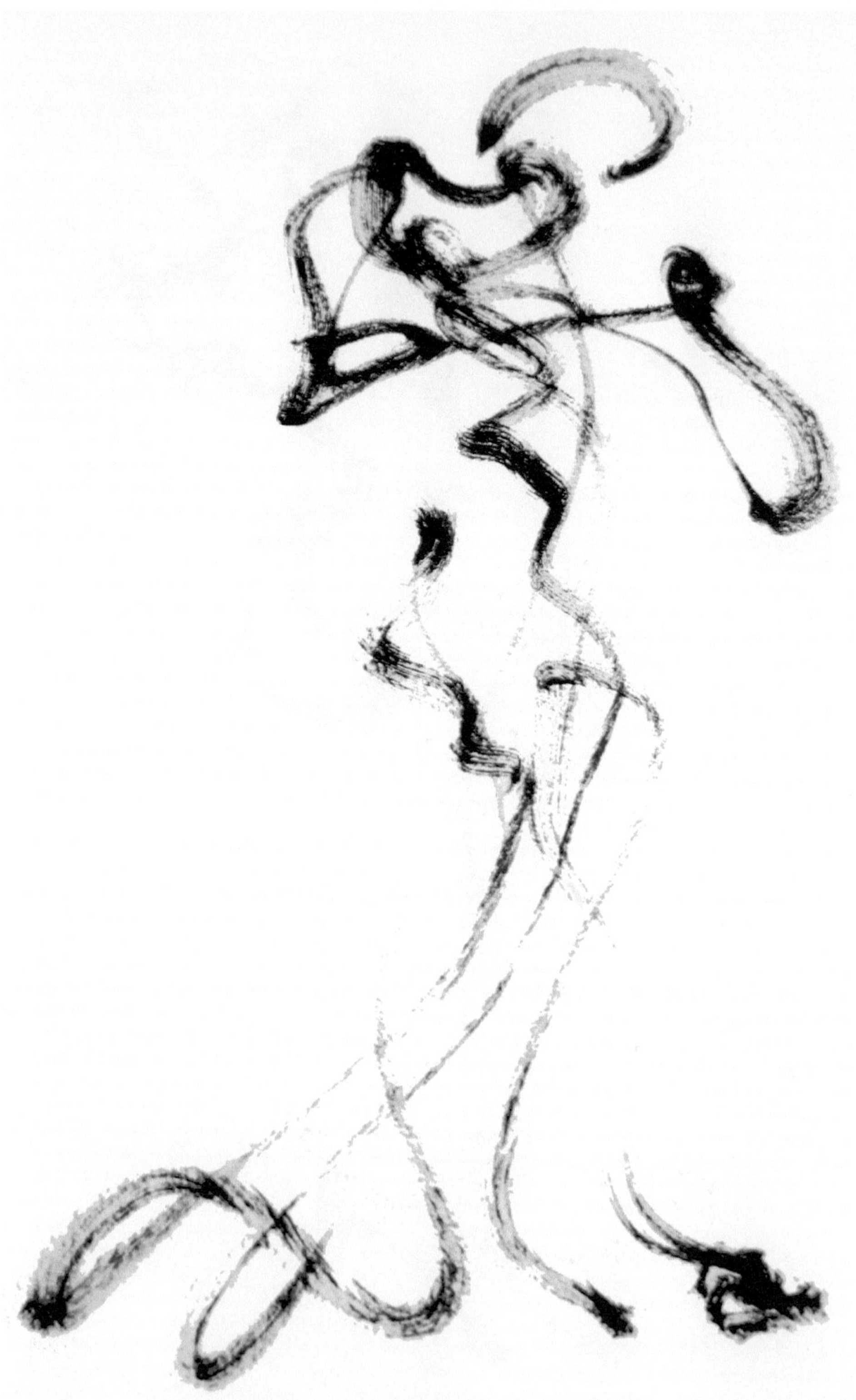

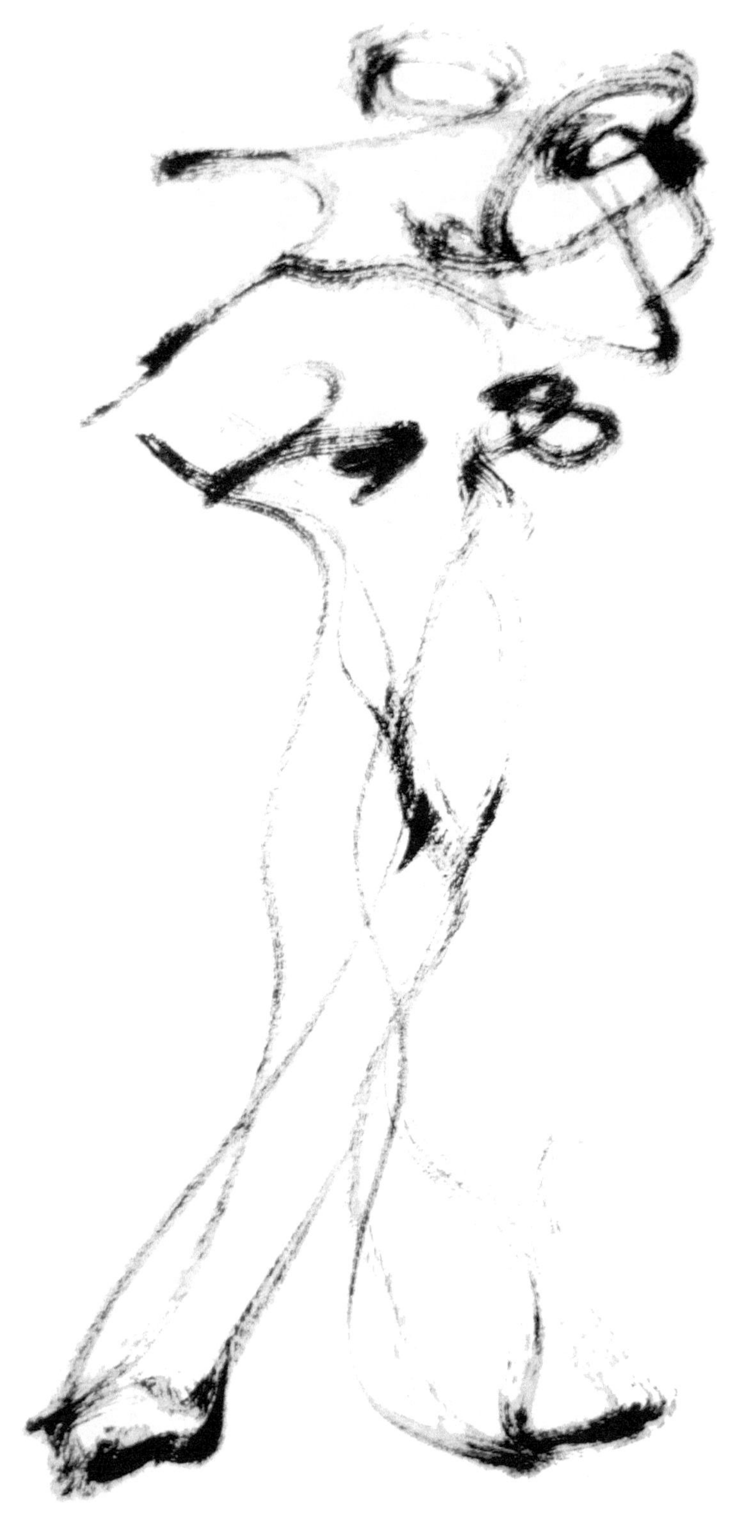

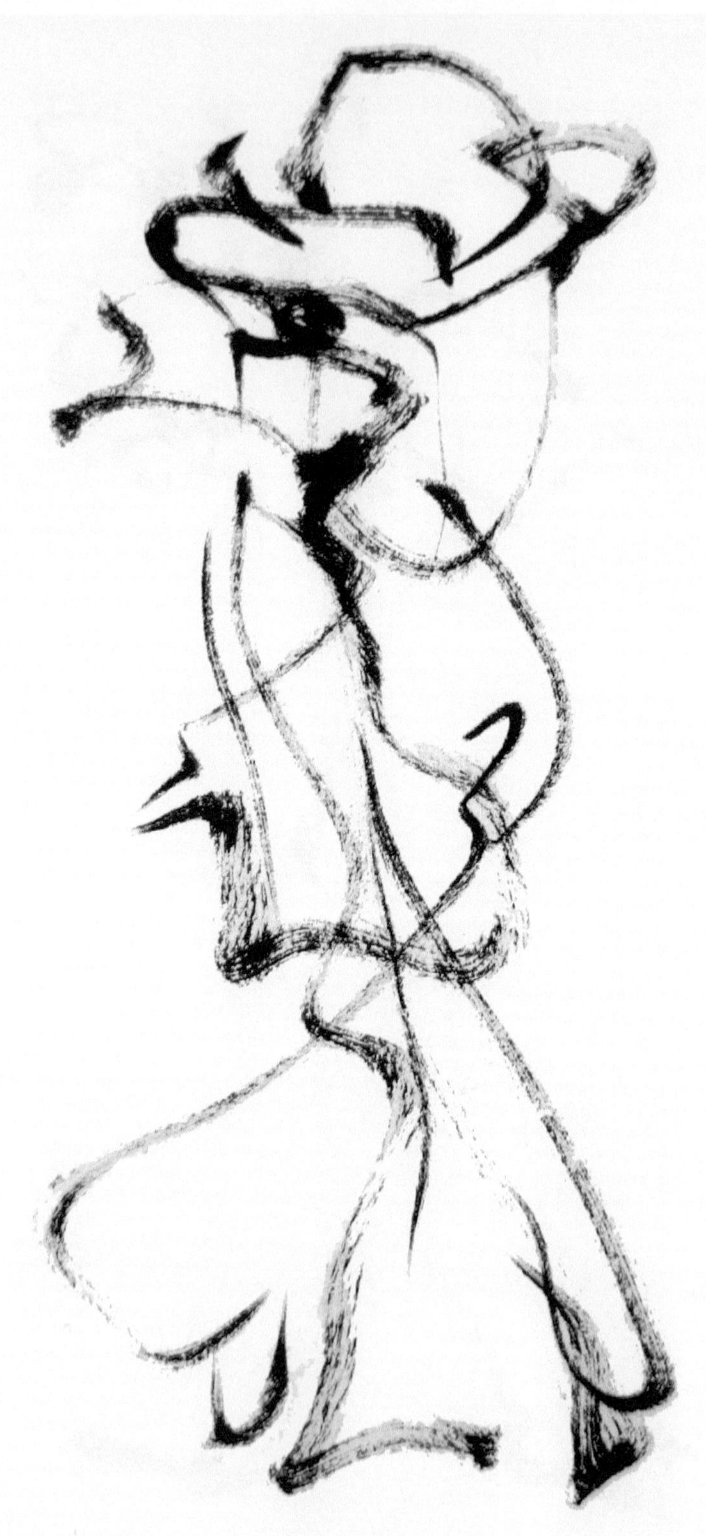

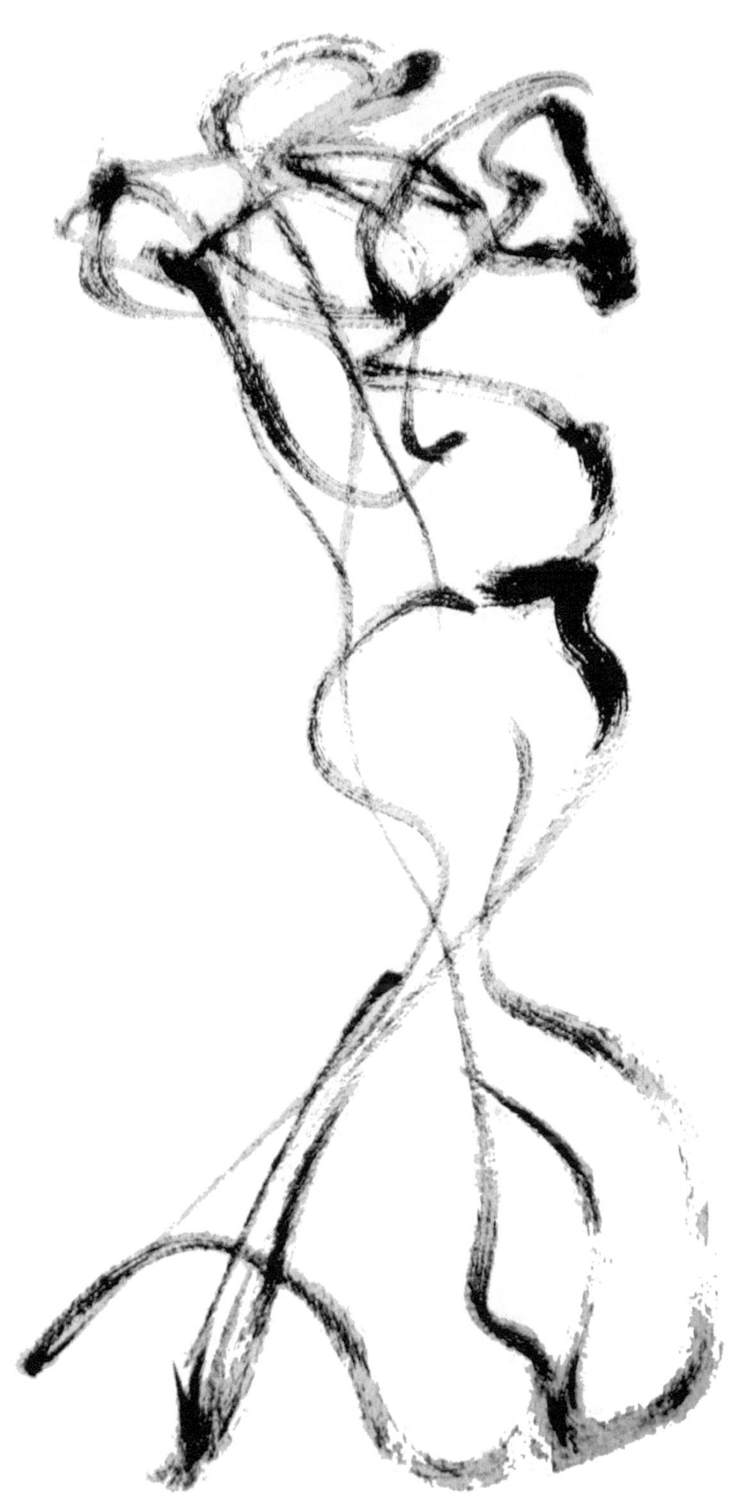

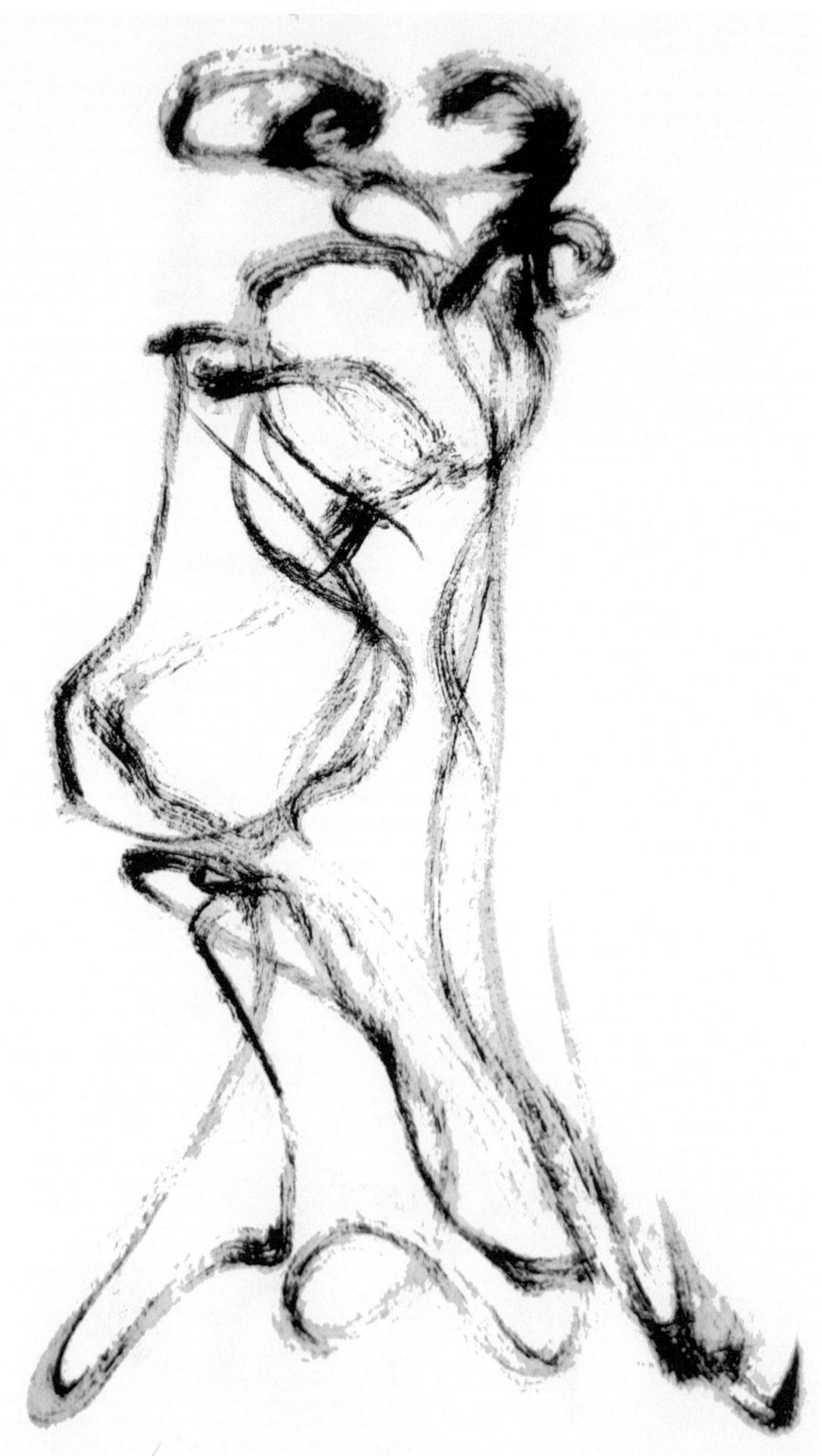

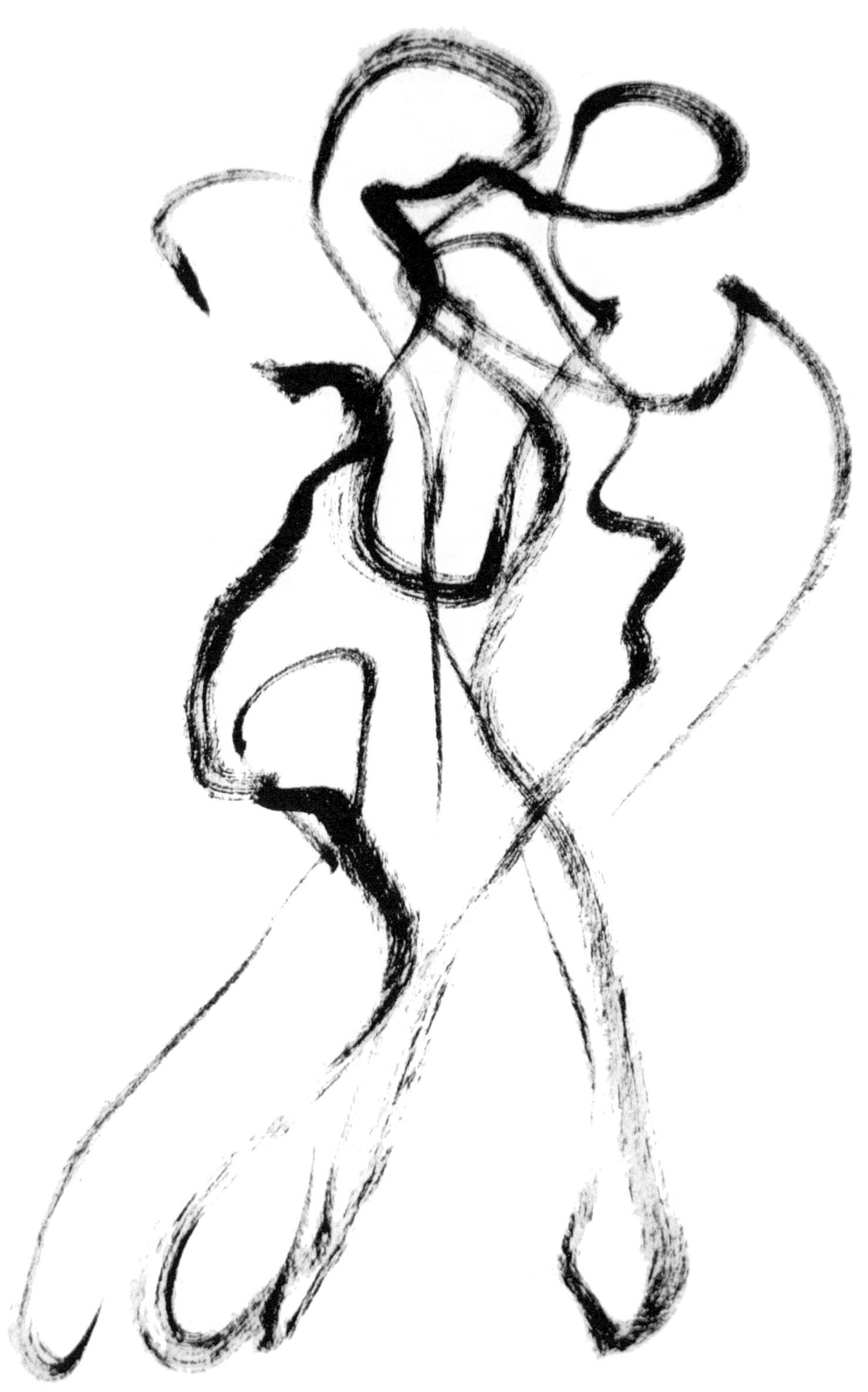

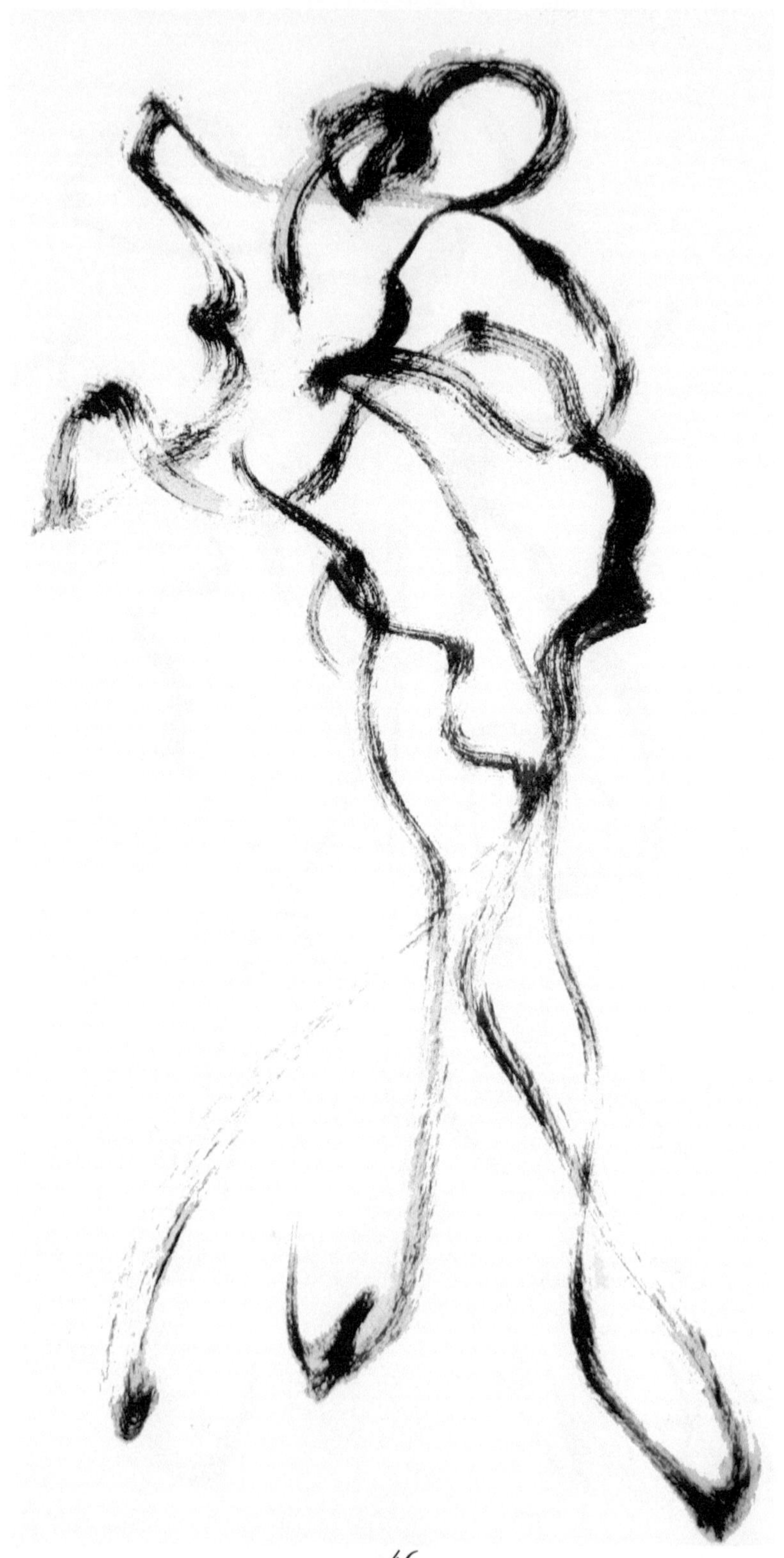

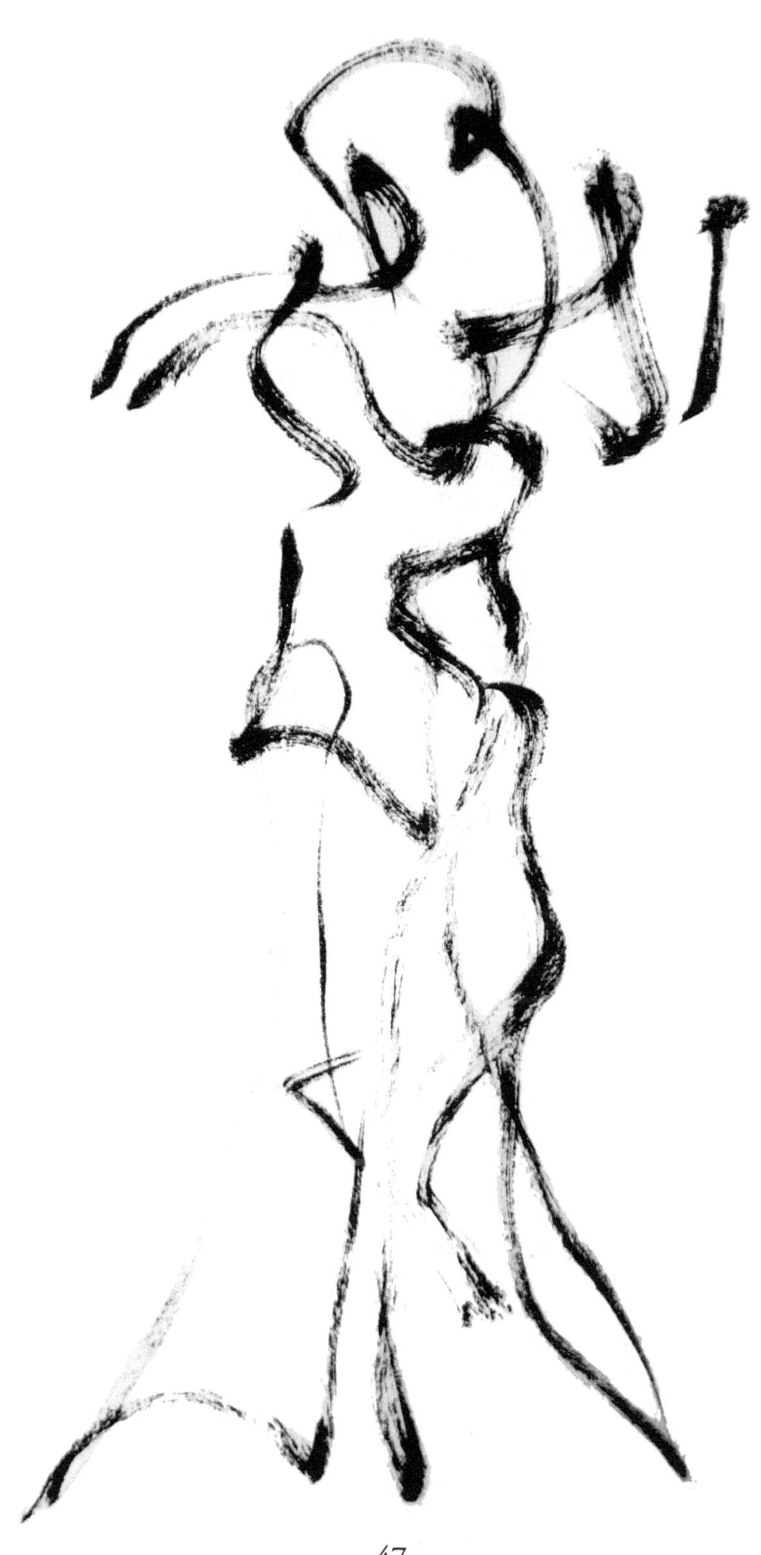

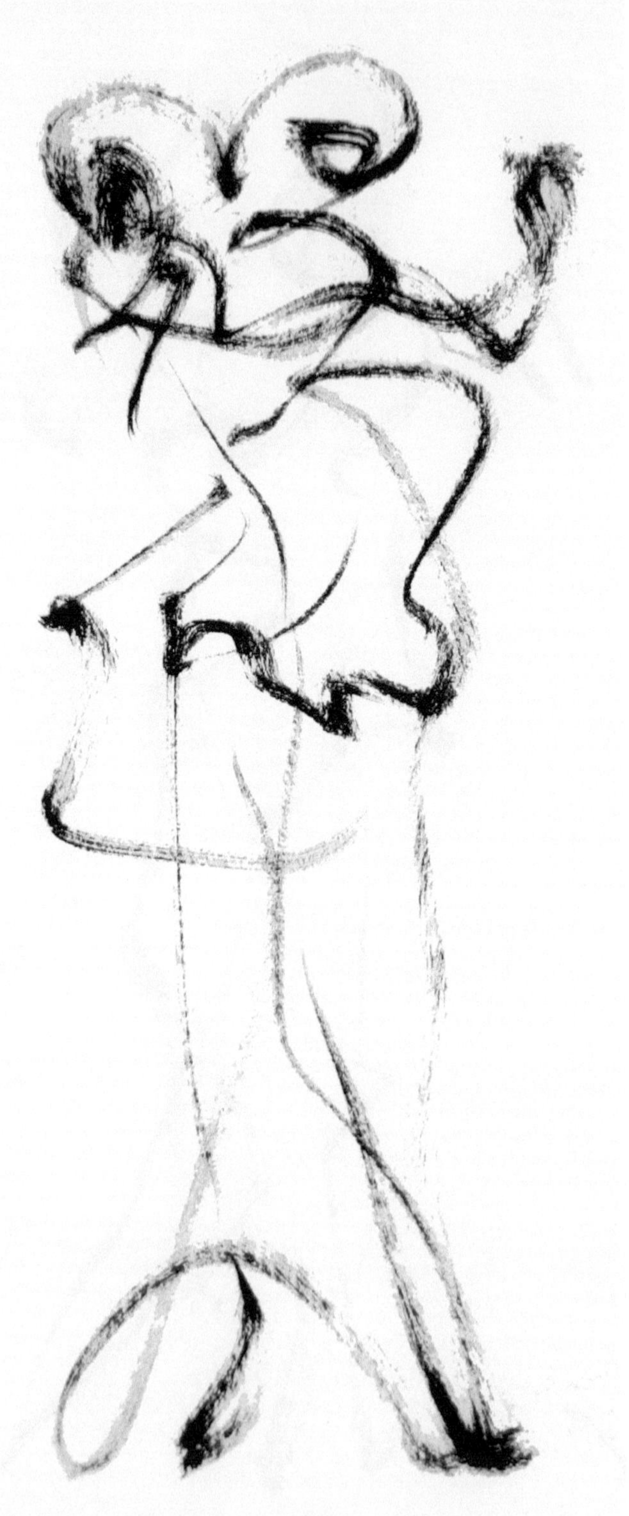

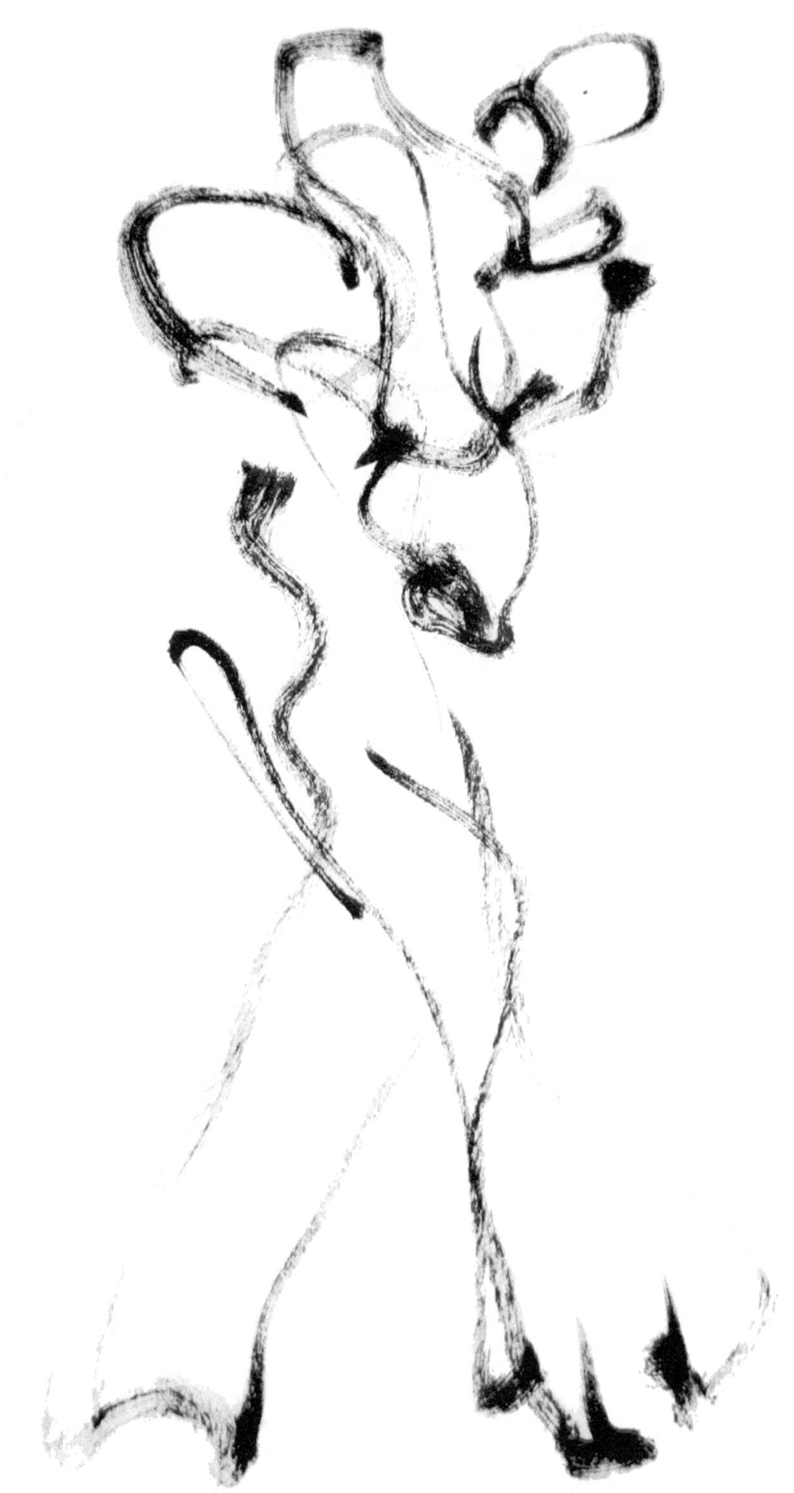

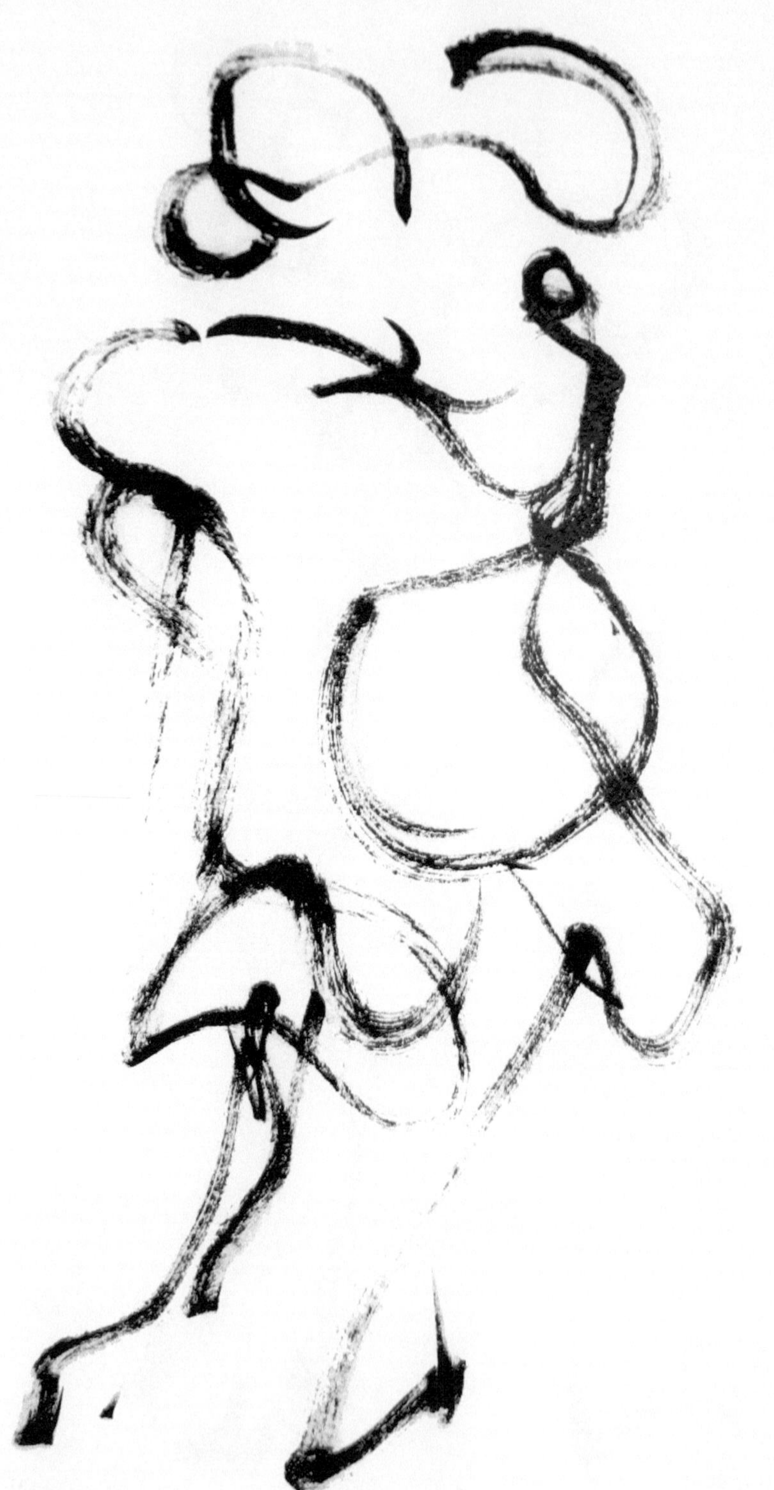

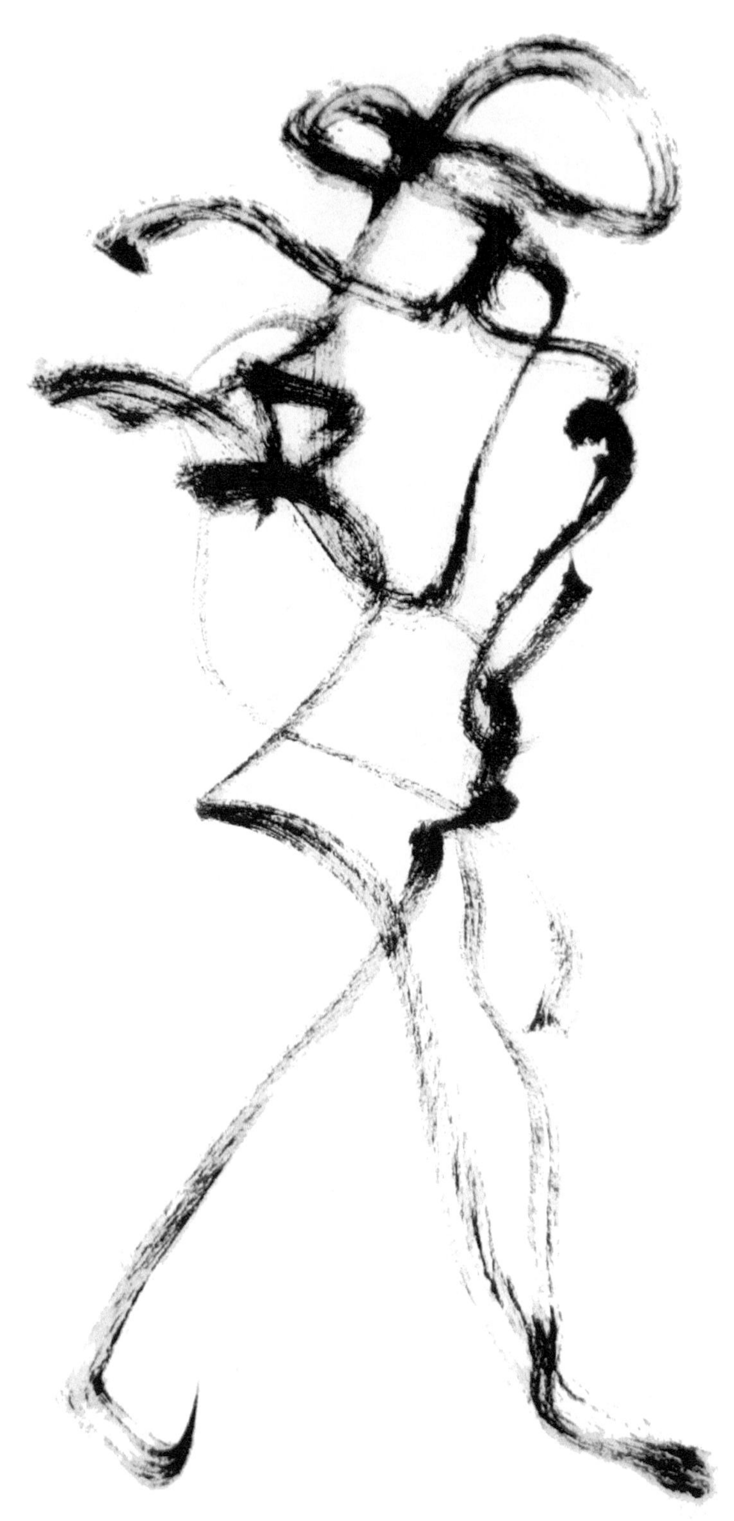

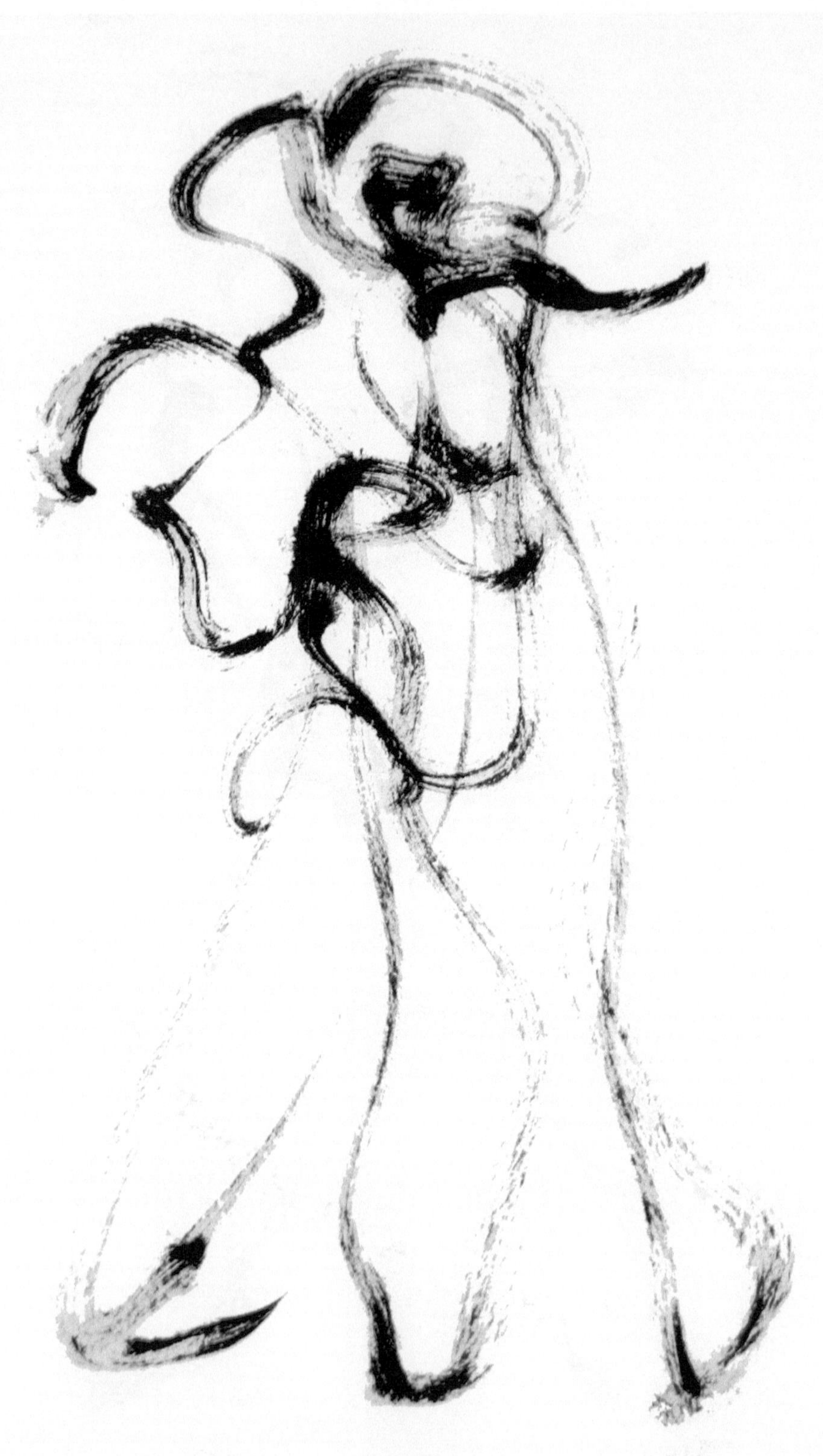

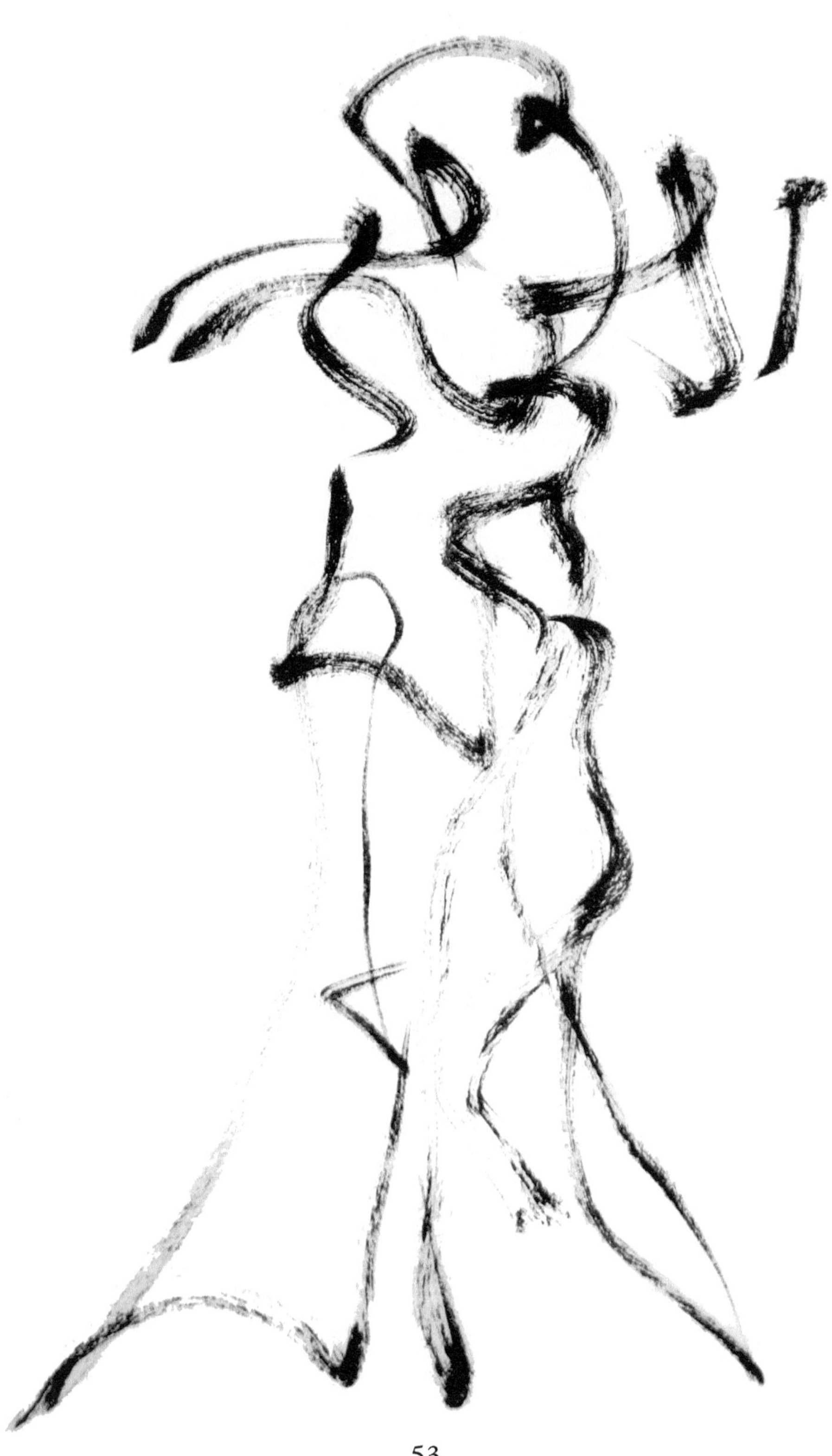

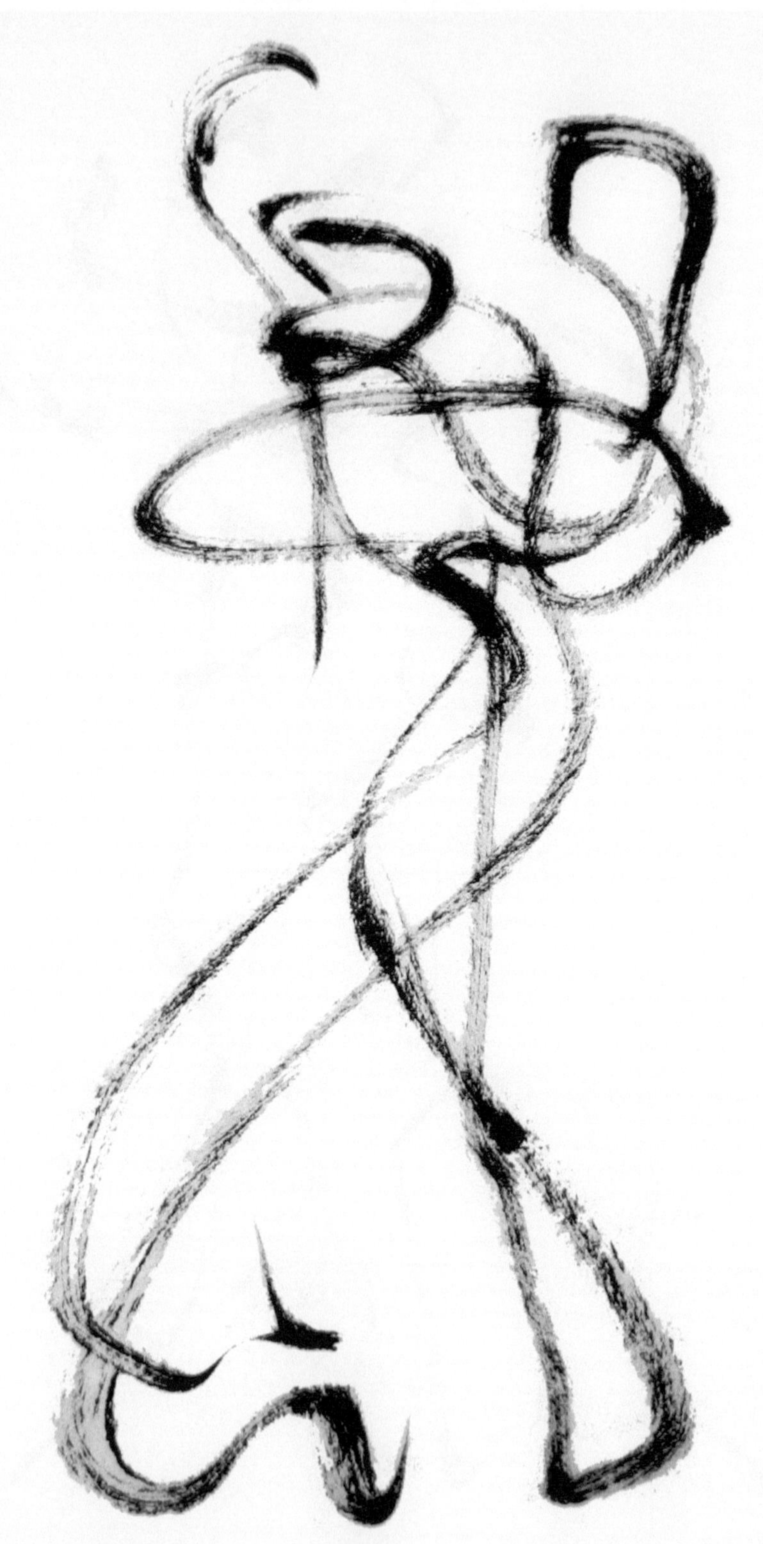

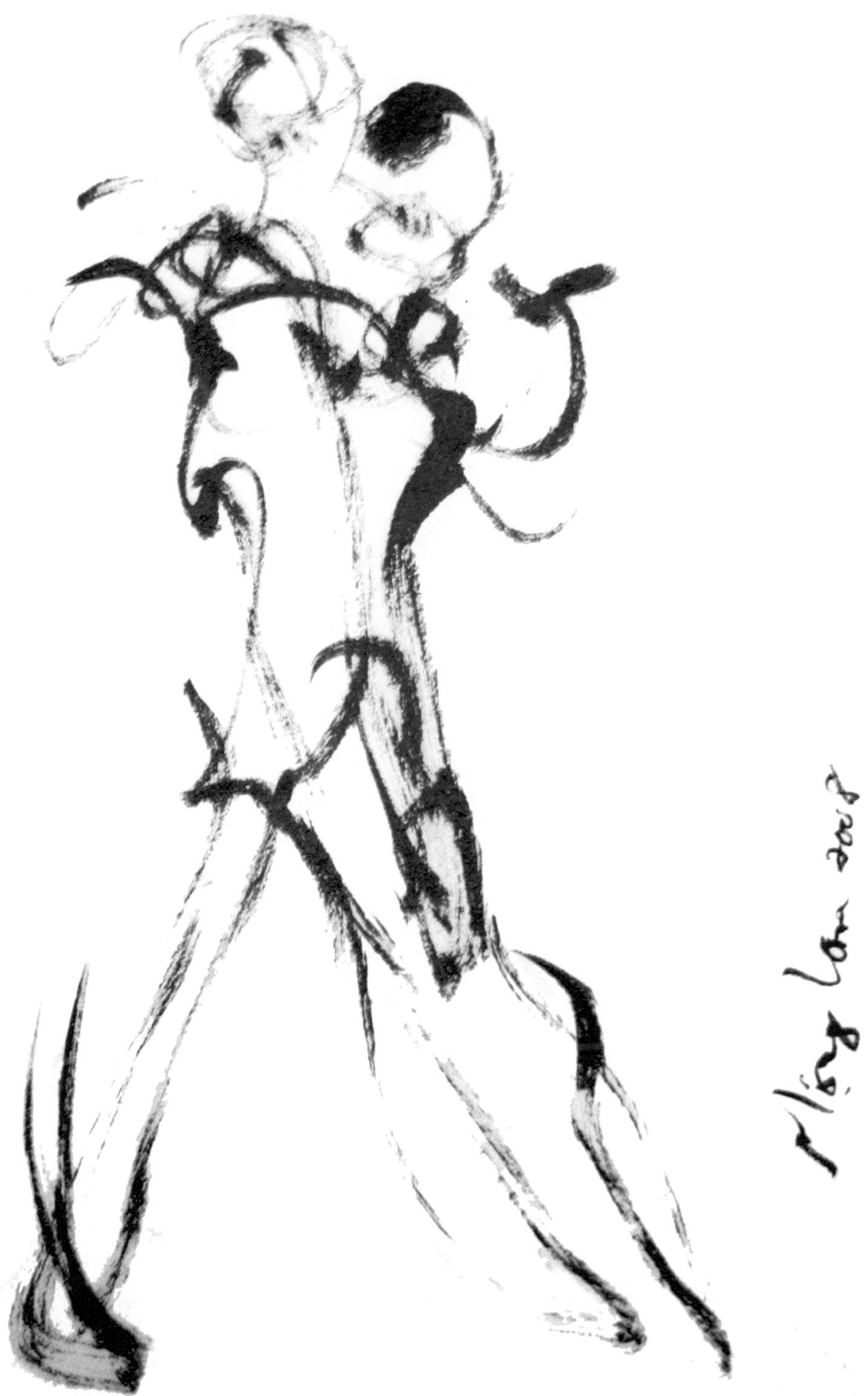

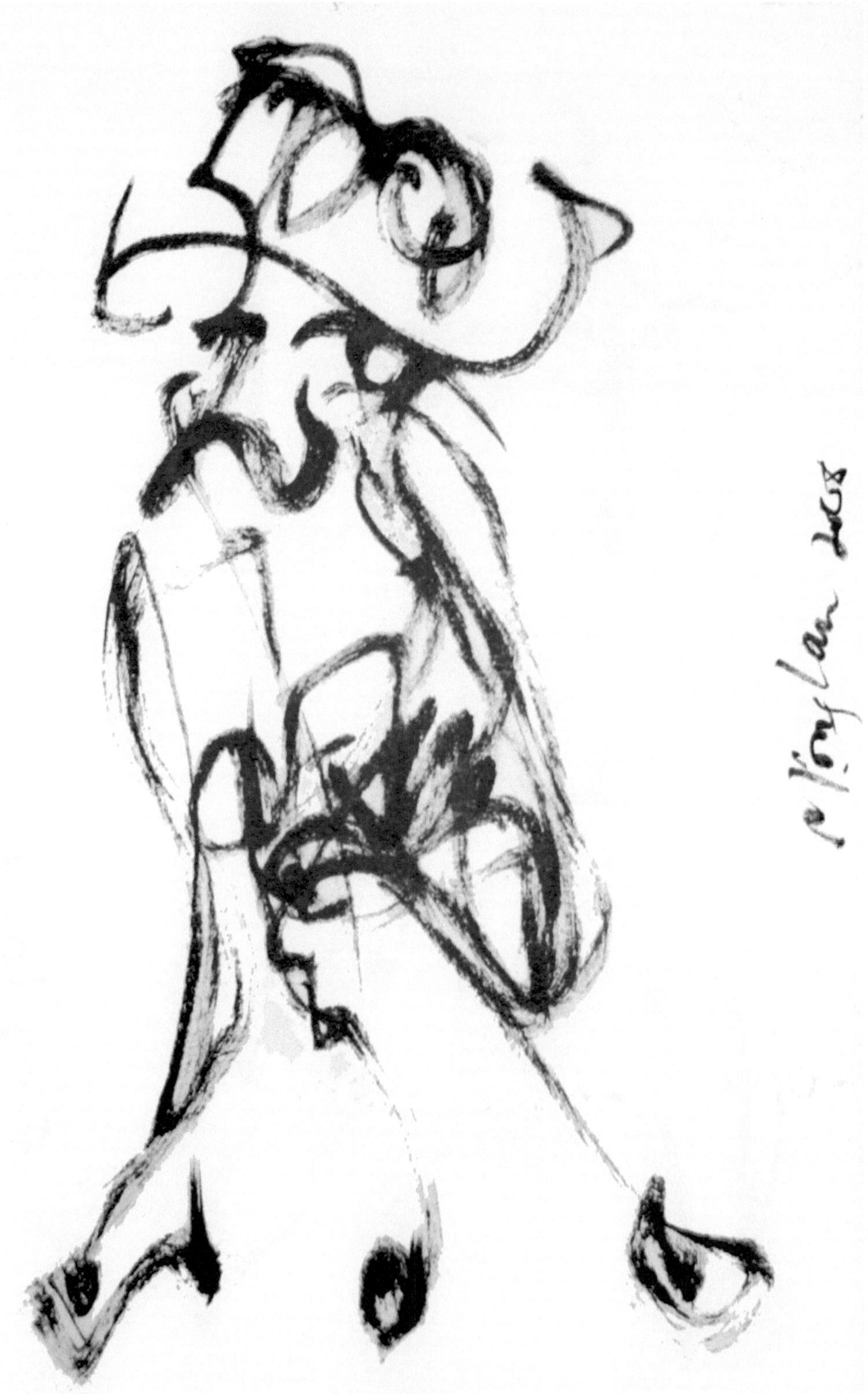

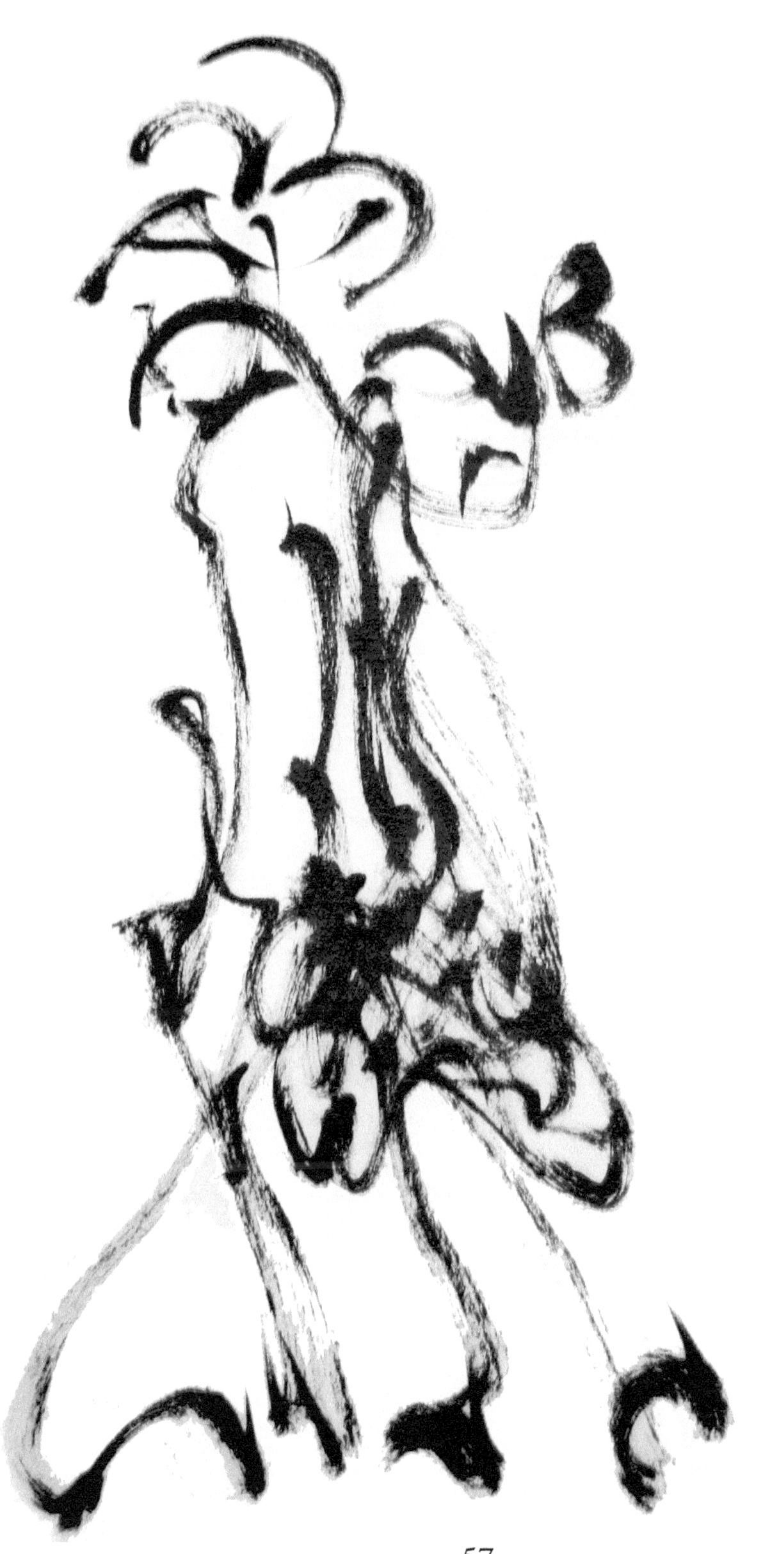

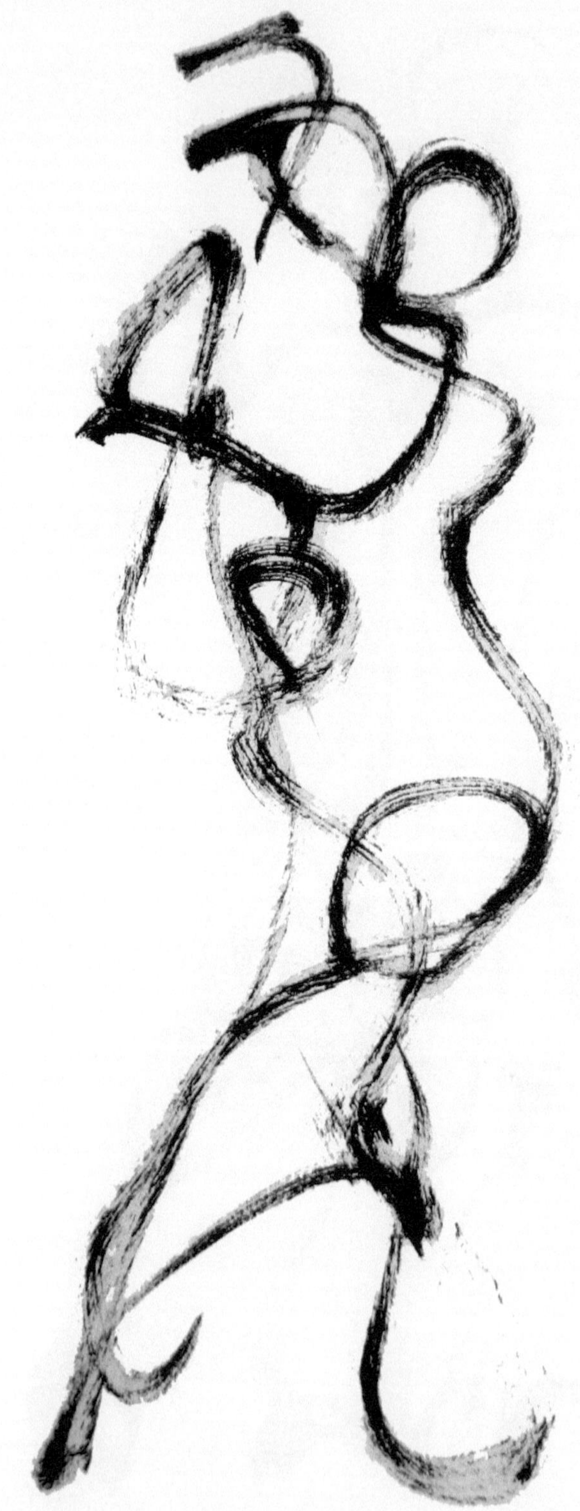

Another day   crossing a bridge of rotted wood   graffiti

quick feet

trains the heart beating

cobbled streets where trolley lines used to run
paved over   still showing the skeletons

a motorcycle burns in the streets

a motorcycle burns

without cause   a motorcycle in flames

how much loss is bearable? how much loss is allowable?

how much love is allowable?

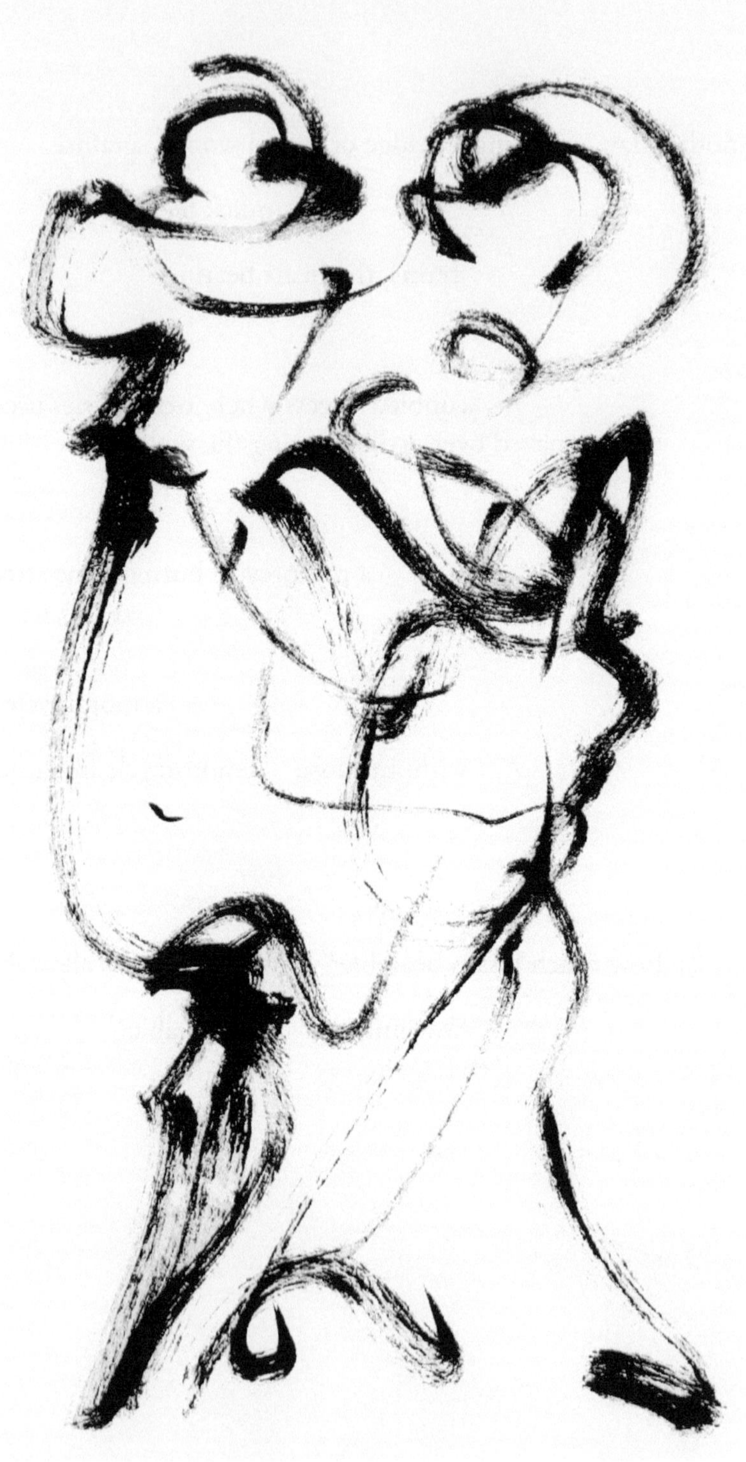

“angustia
de sentirme abandonado
y pensar que otro a su lado . . . .”

a car burnt to the ground

the disappearing act   into air

then you disappeared   through the forest

of my heart

must i stay with the tango for you? my heart, ravenous. my veins, long highways i traverse to get to you. i am outside of time. being outside of time, i am closer to you. being outside, i get used to being outside. i have always been there.

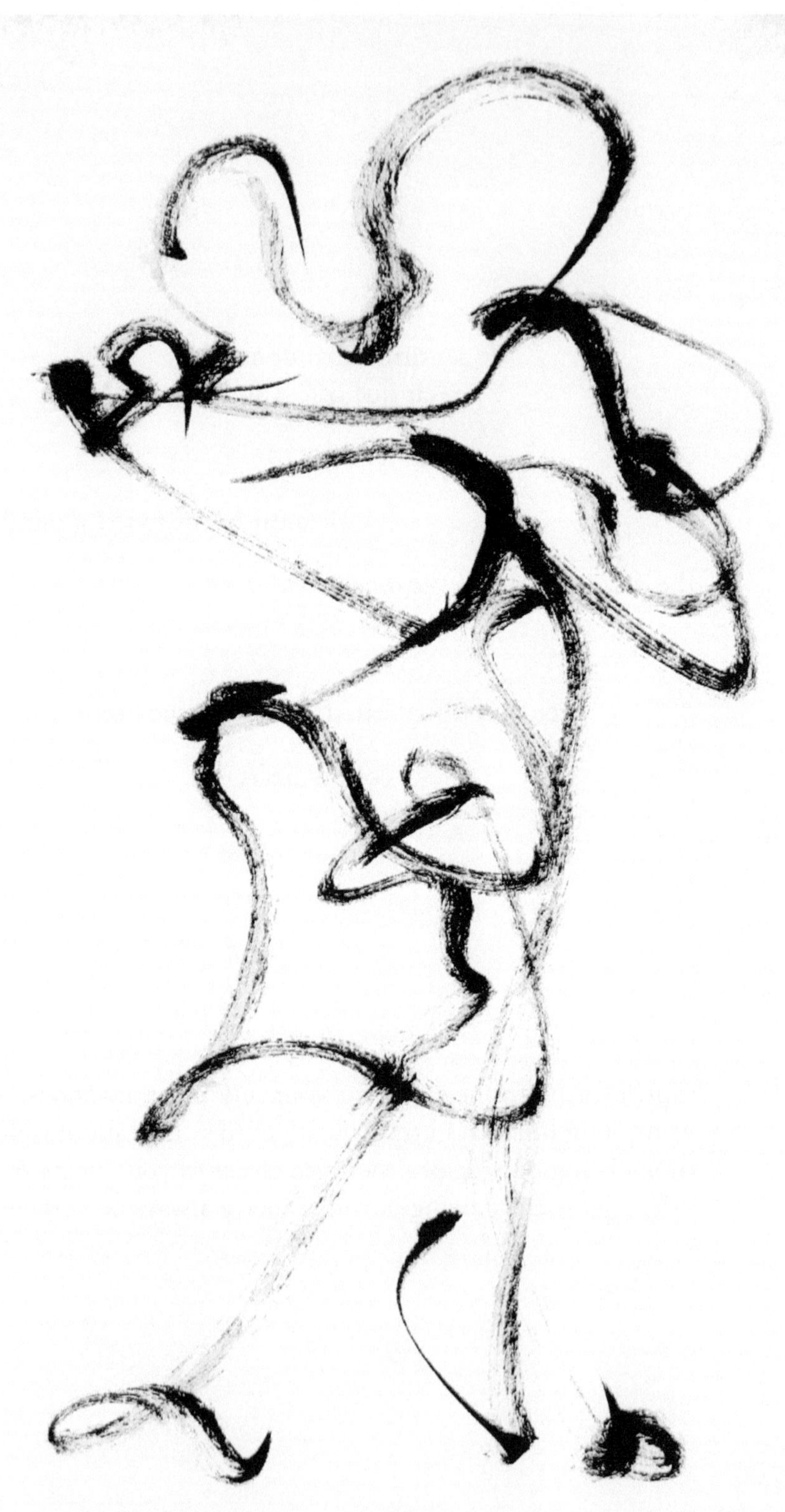

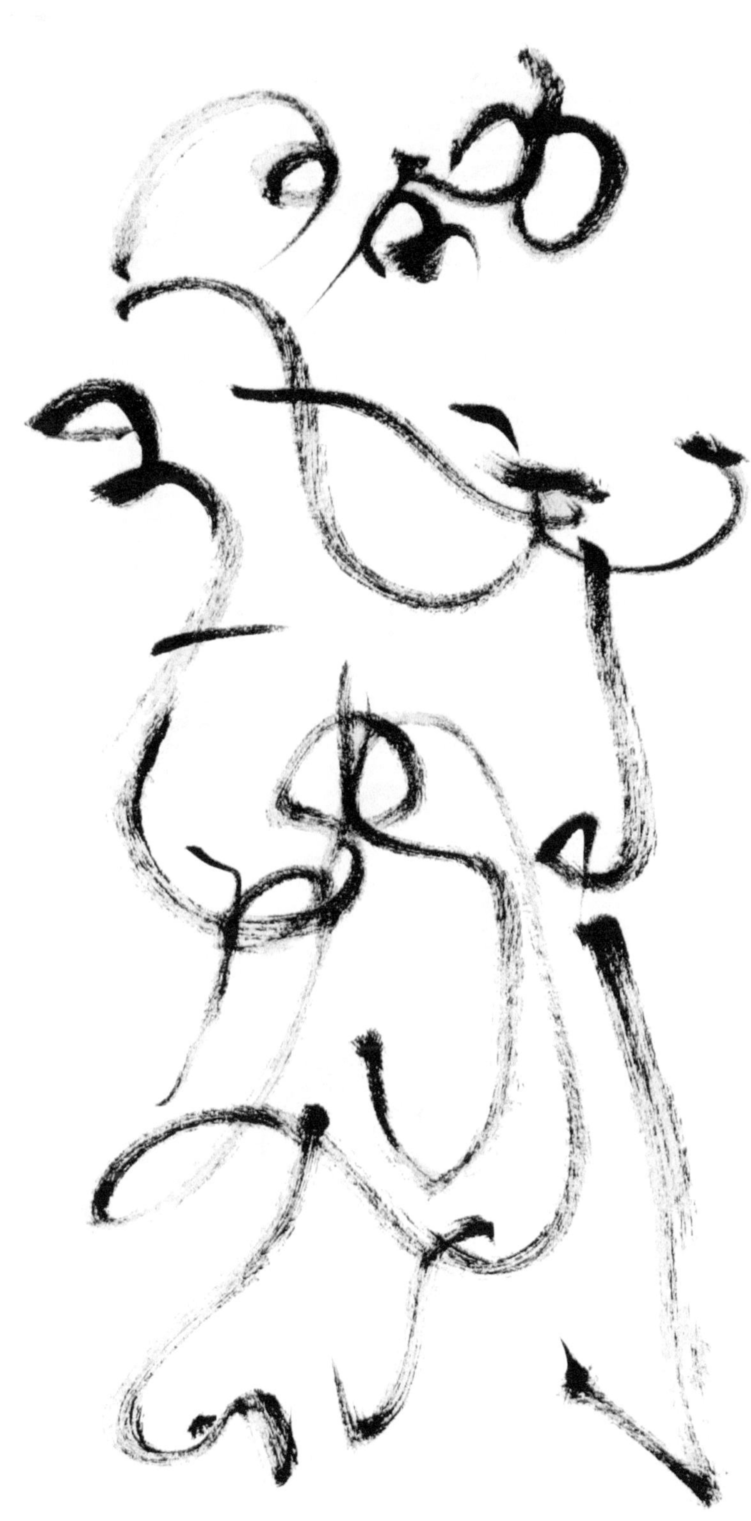

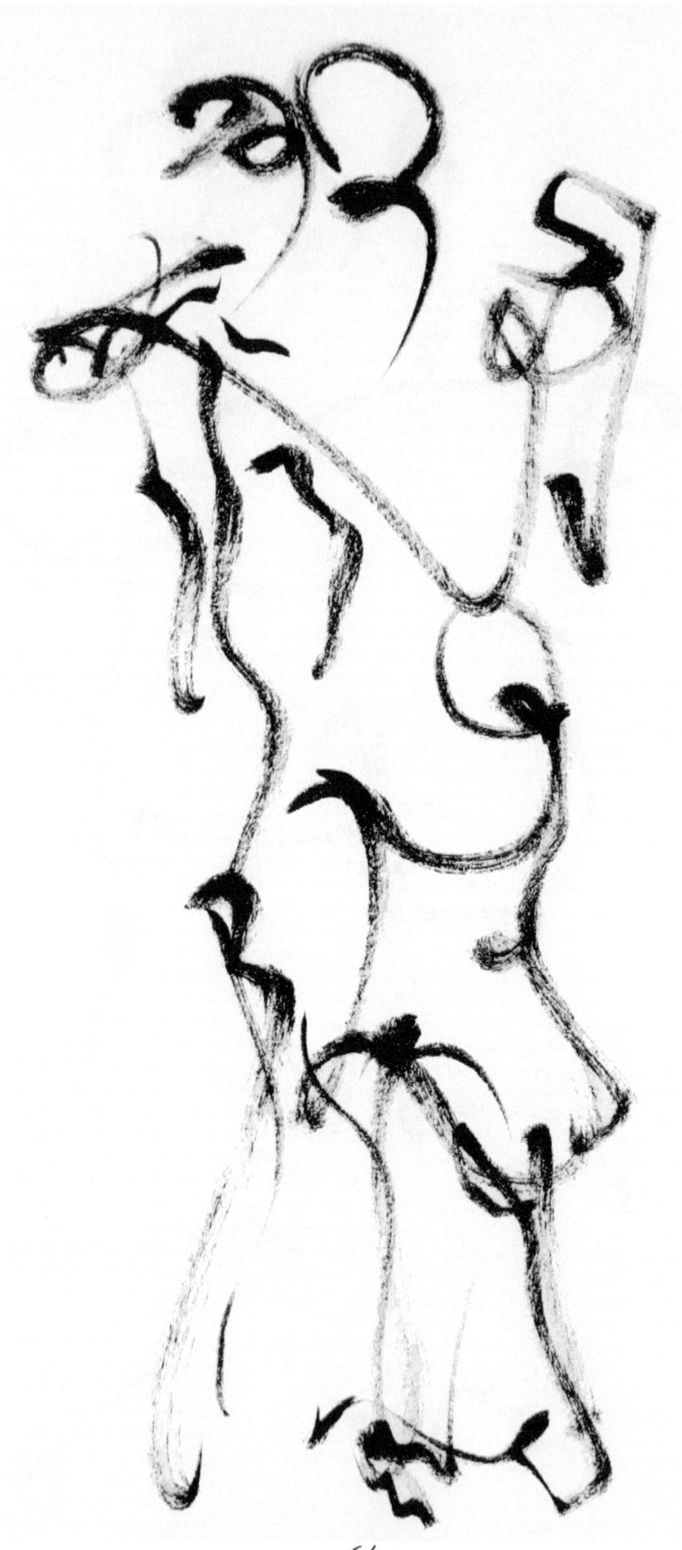

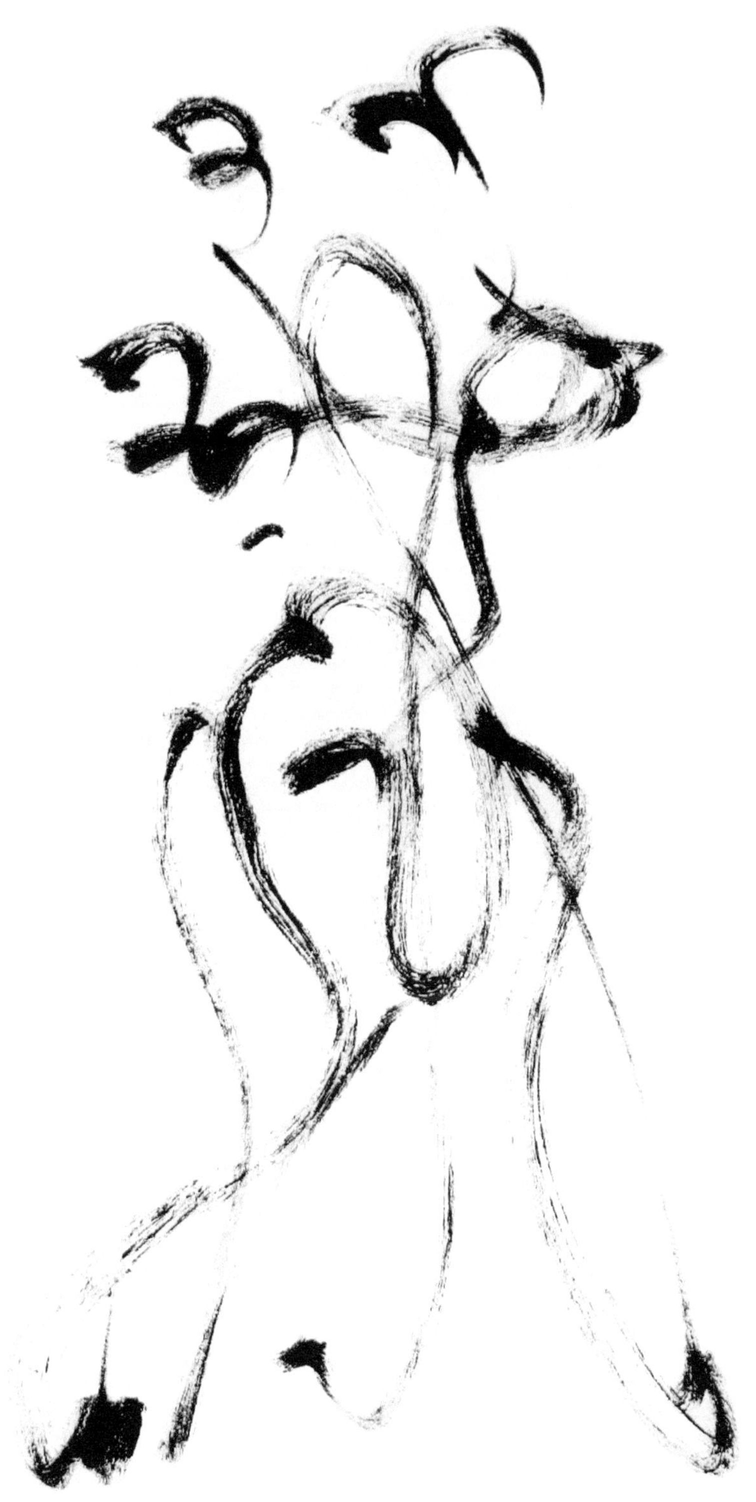

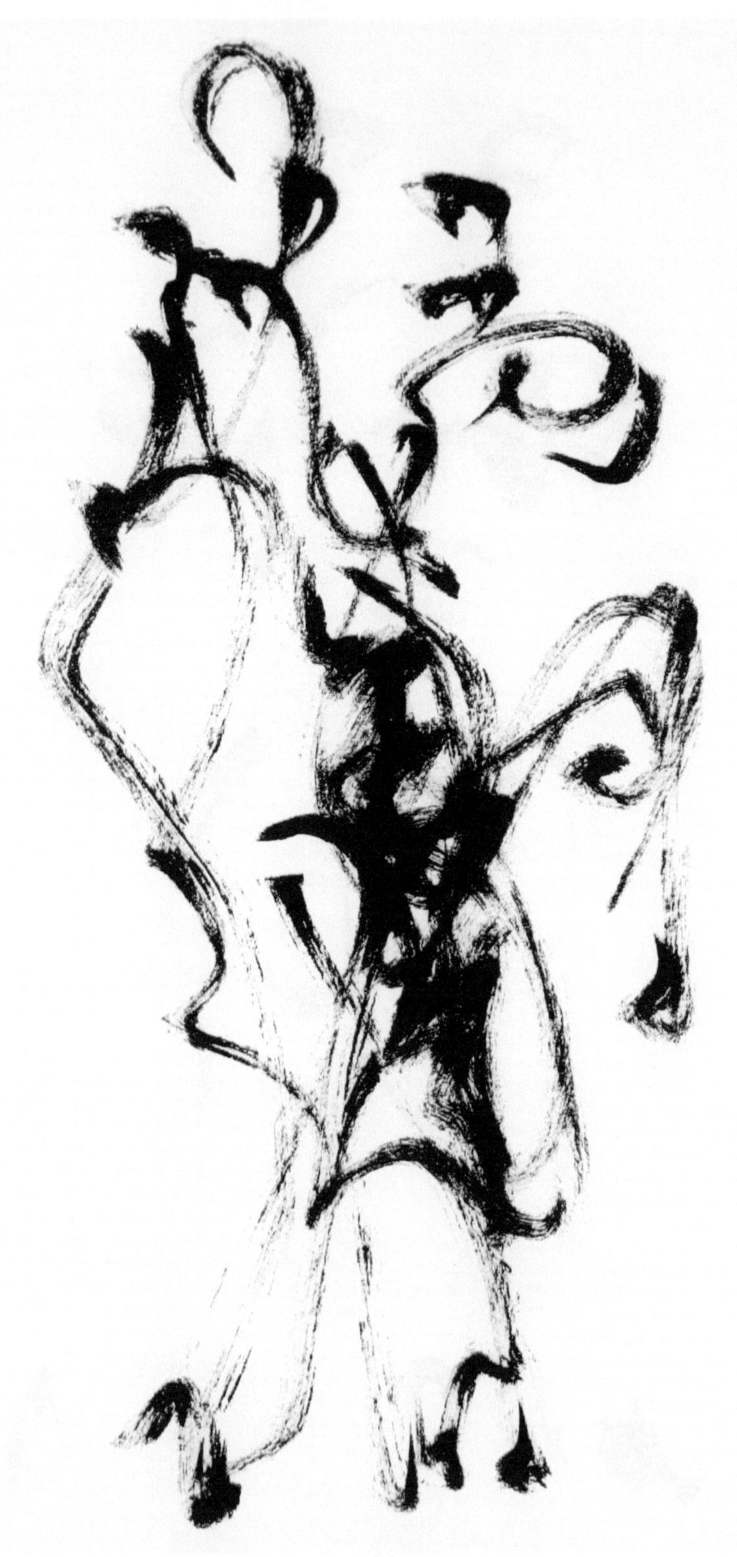

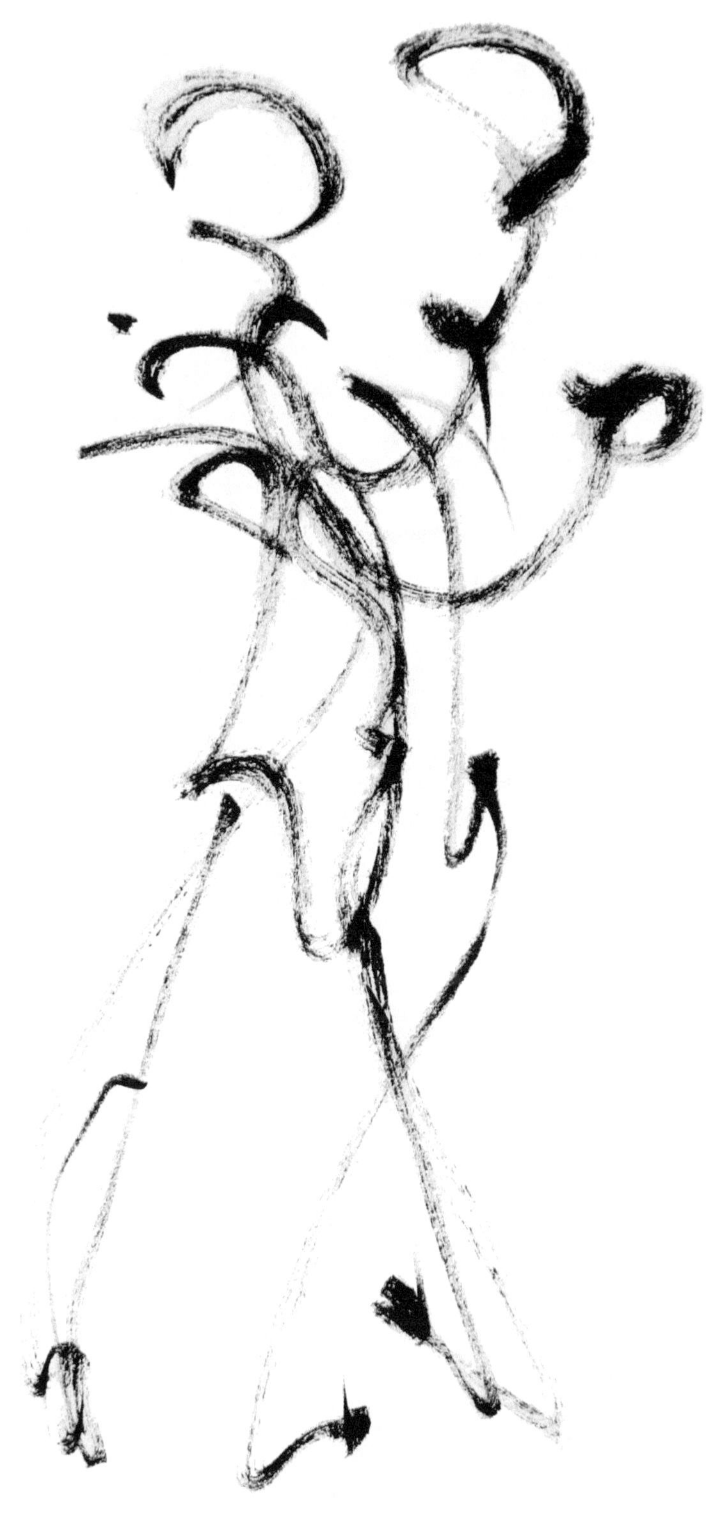

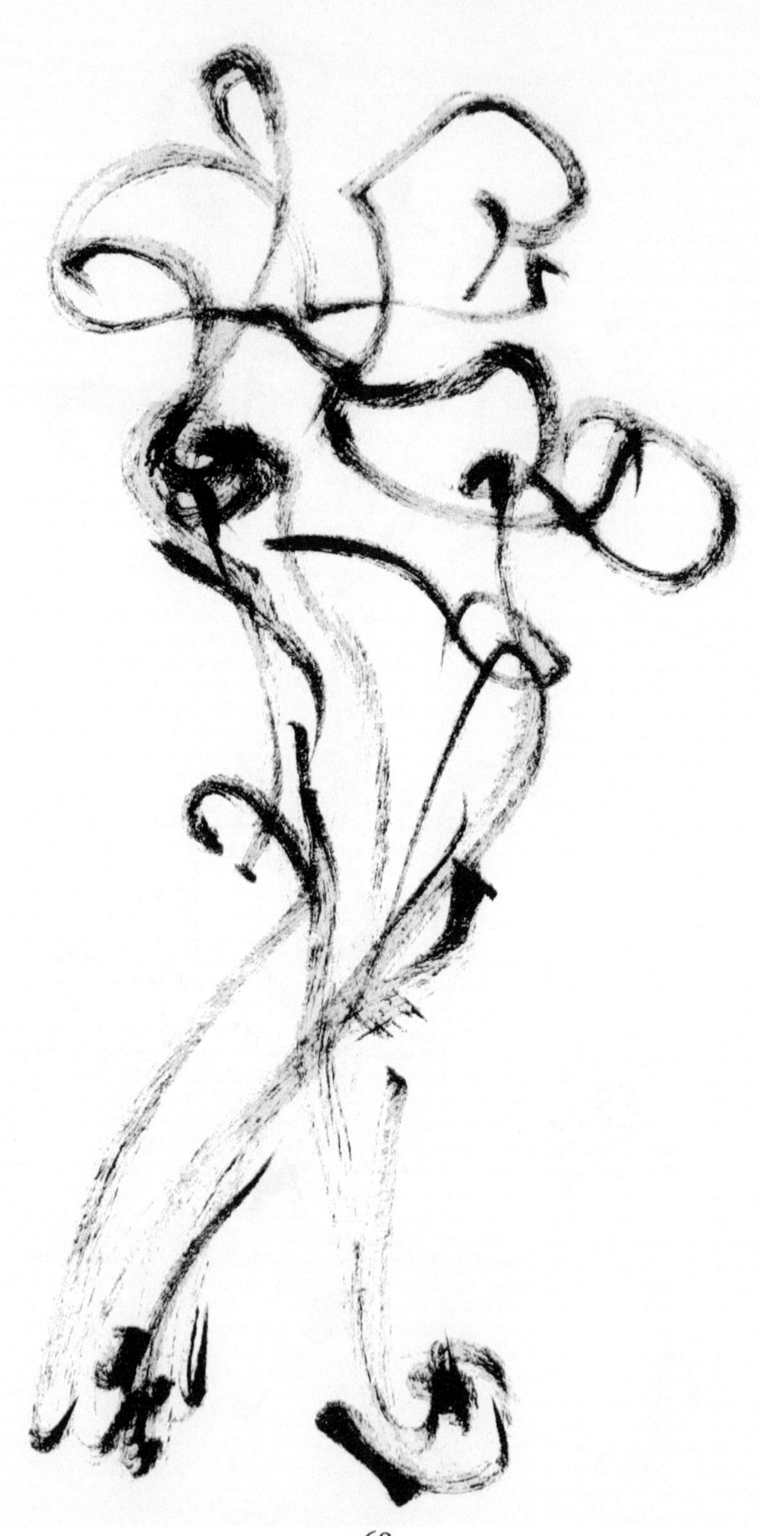

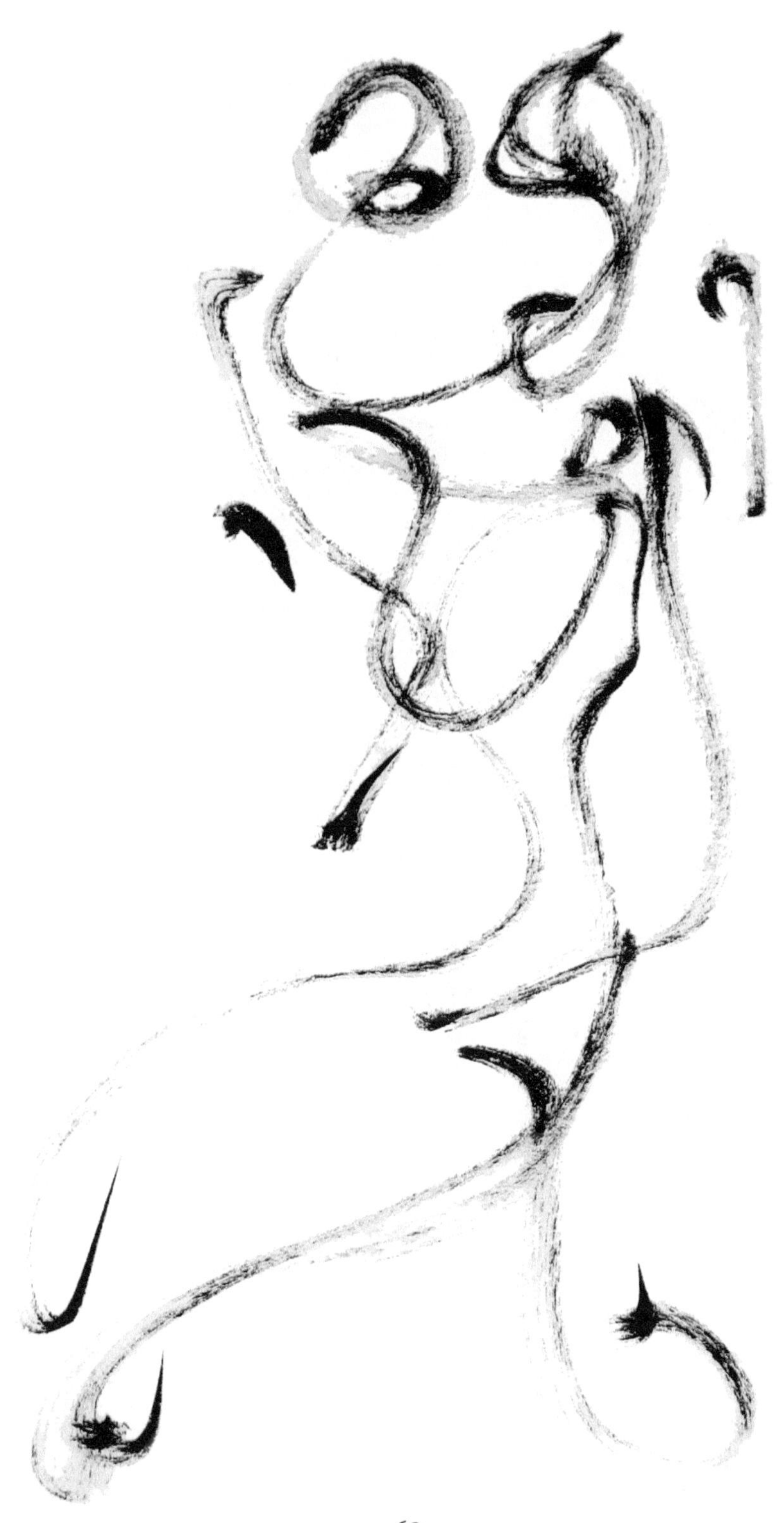

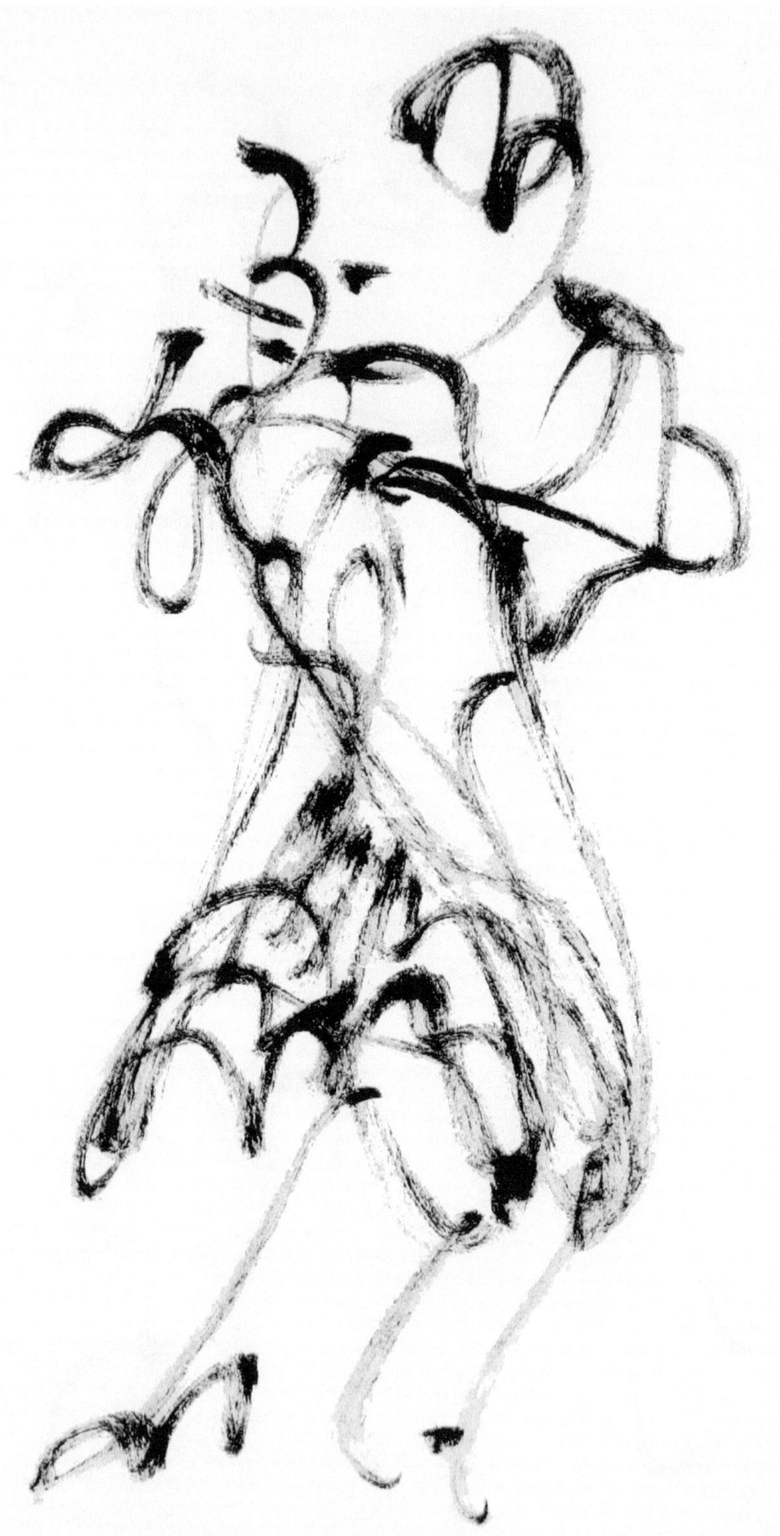

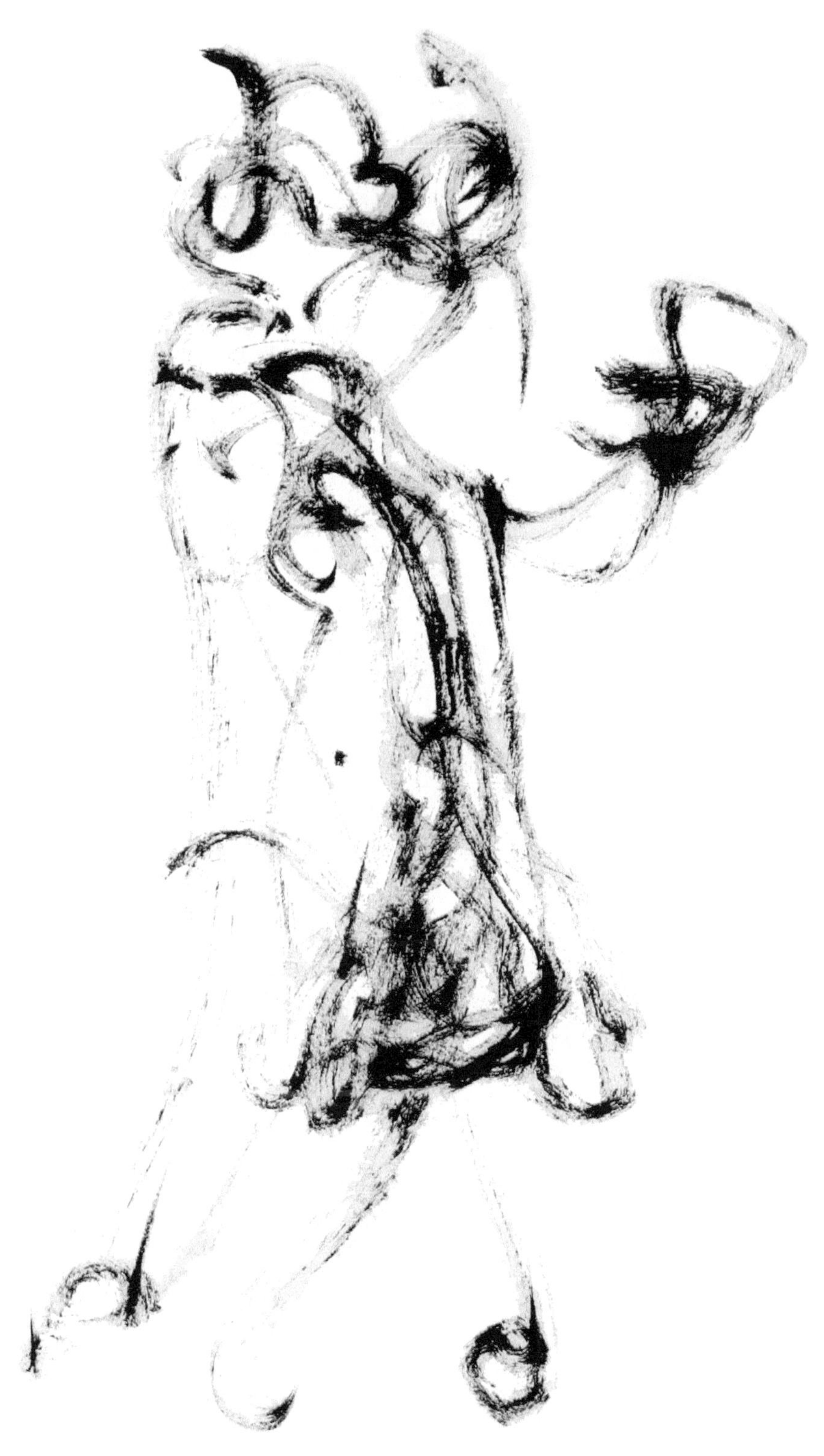

sucking a fish eye i taste the ocean

sucking a fish fin i swim with the fish

it's meteorological . . . .

meteorical

you enveloped me all
of you

your scent so slight

constantly i'm in your embrace it will happen again

one day without you my love and all days
break

one day without you my love

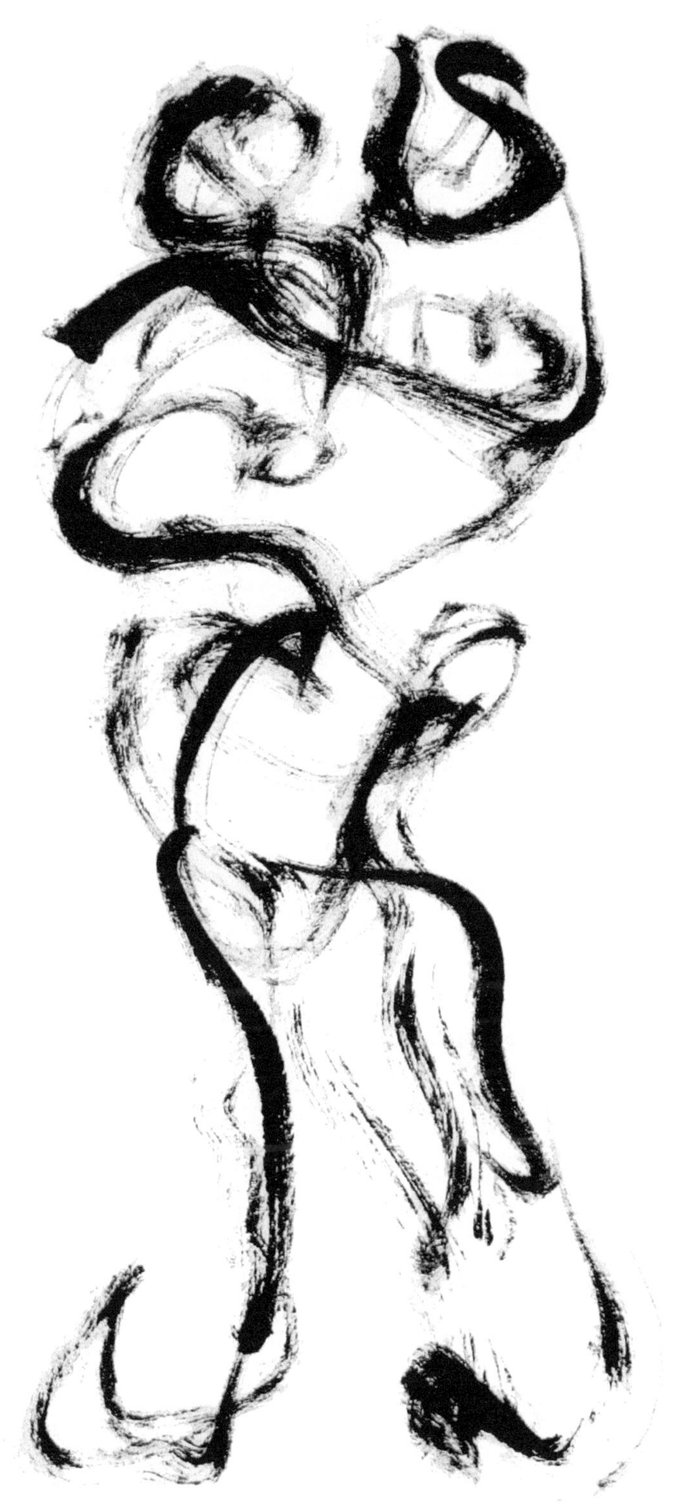

"las calles y las lunas surbanas

y mi amor y tu ventana . . . ."

~

a man will keep cheating on his wife. the *milonguero* continues to have many lovers. he is married to the tango, his real wife. the woman herself does not matter—she could be anyone. she can be remarkably dim, and it will most likely be fine for the tango man. her body matters most, not her soul, nor her mind. a body is replaceable; it is merely a body.

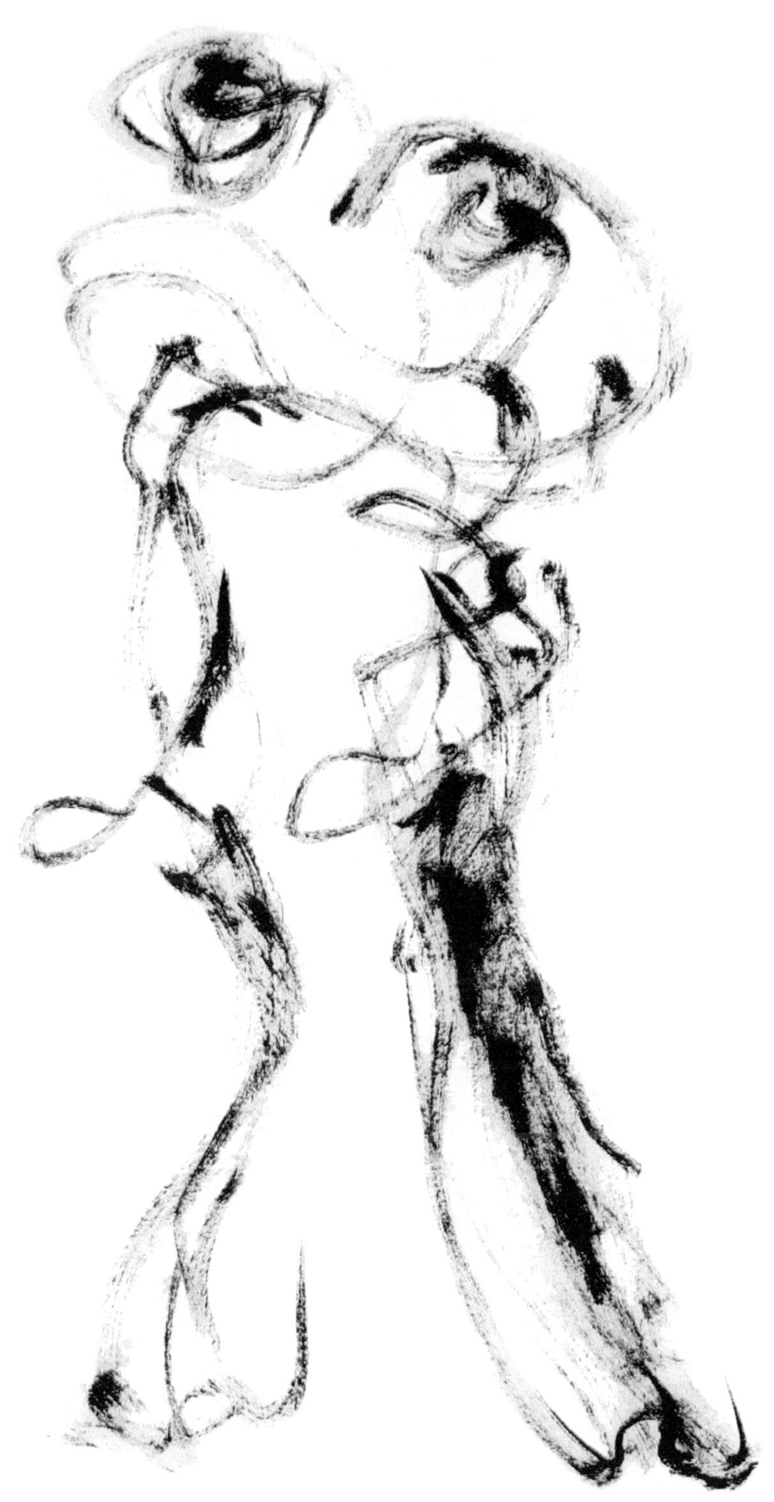

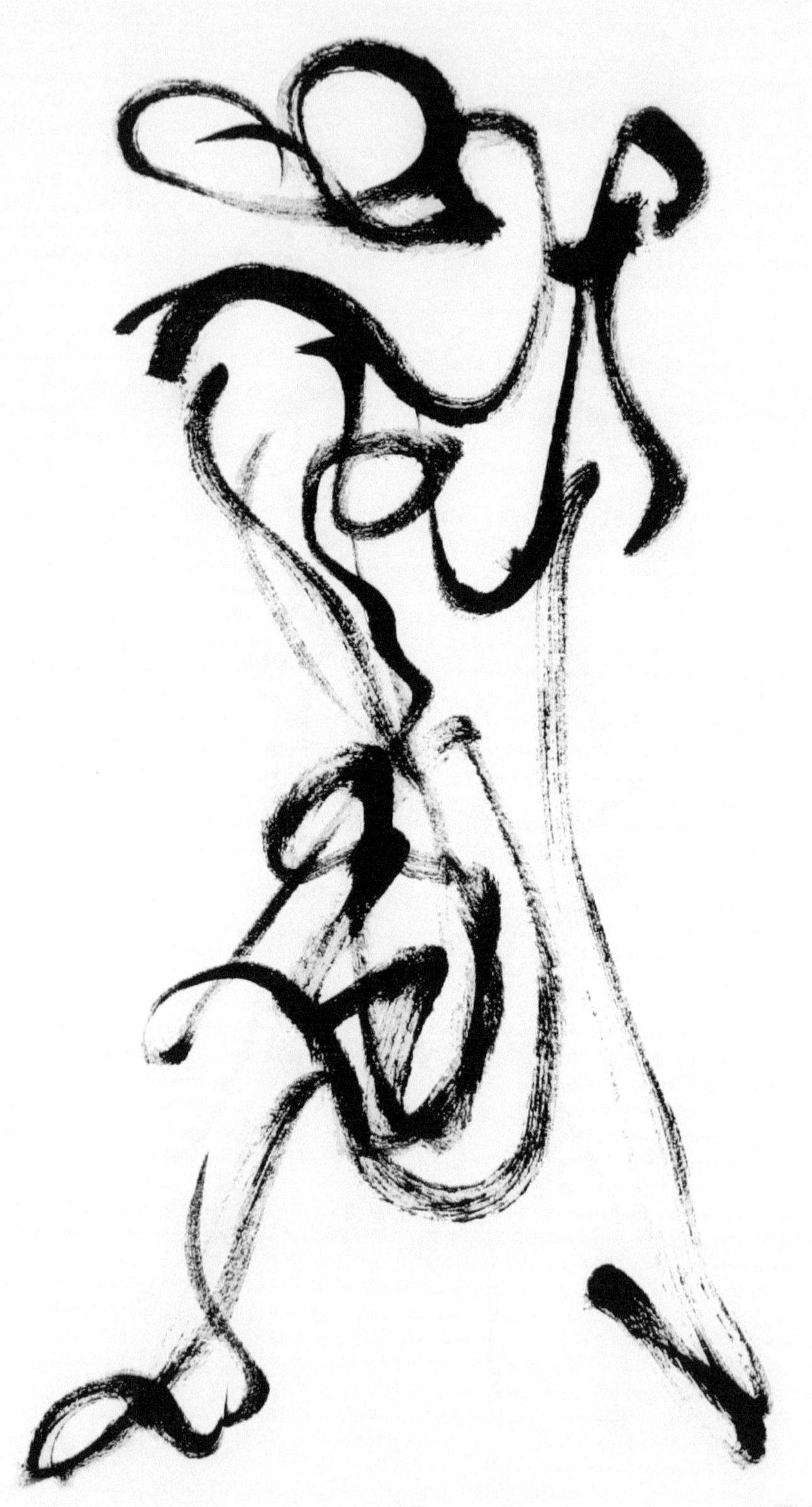

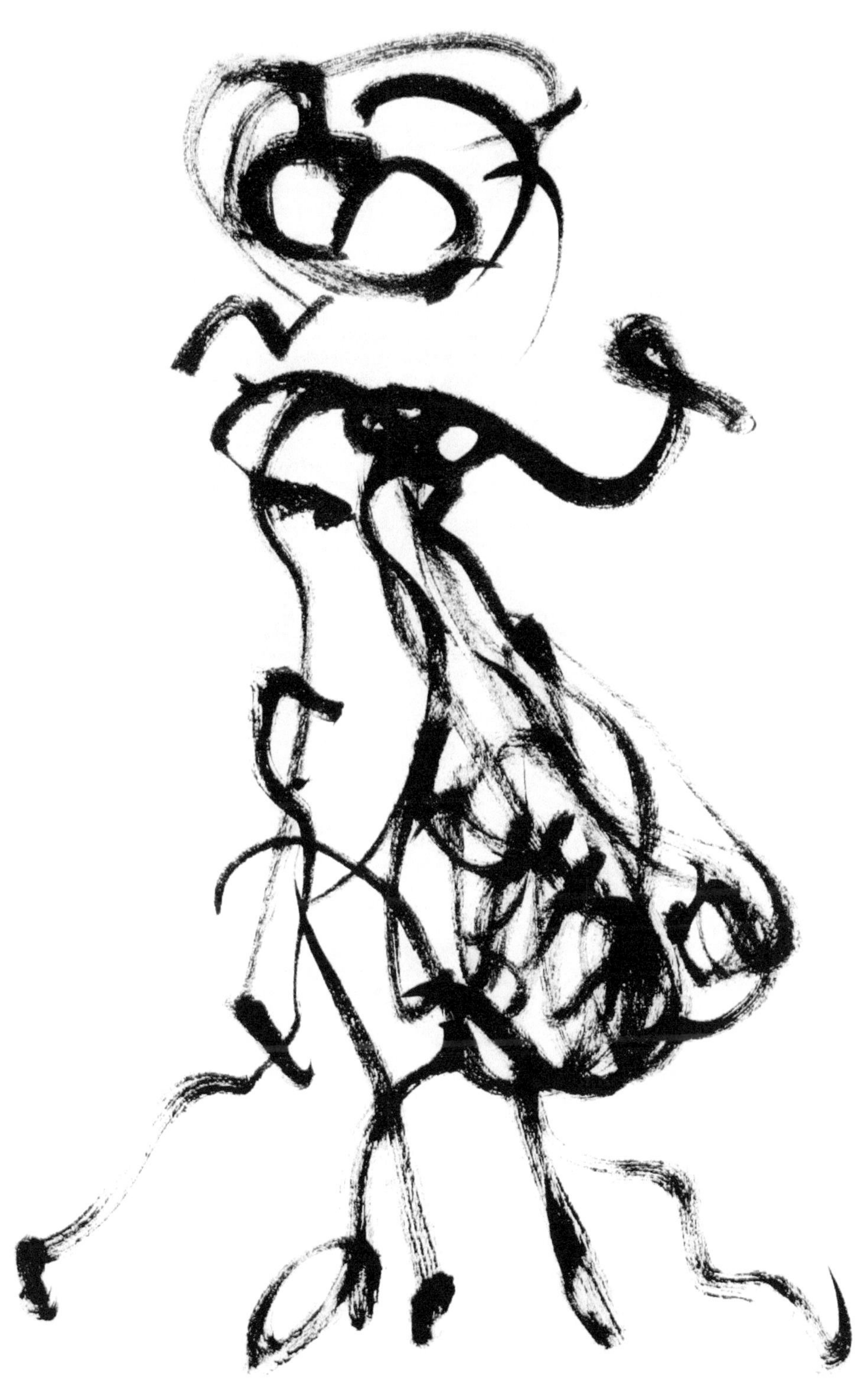

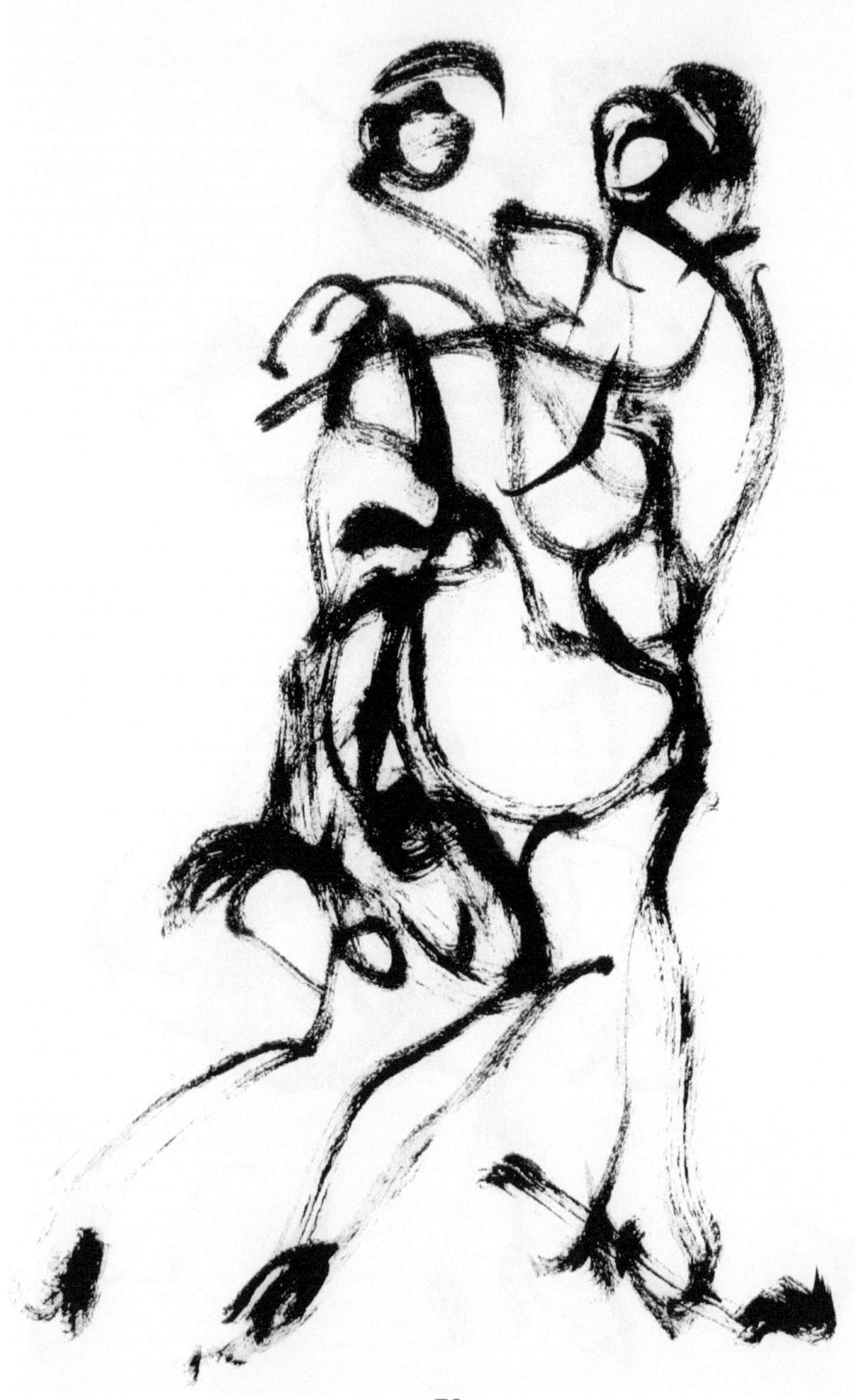

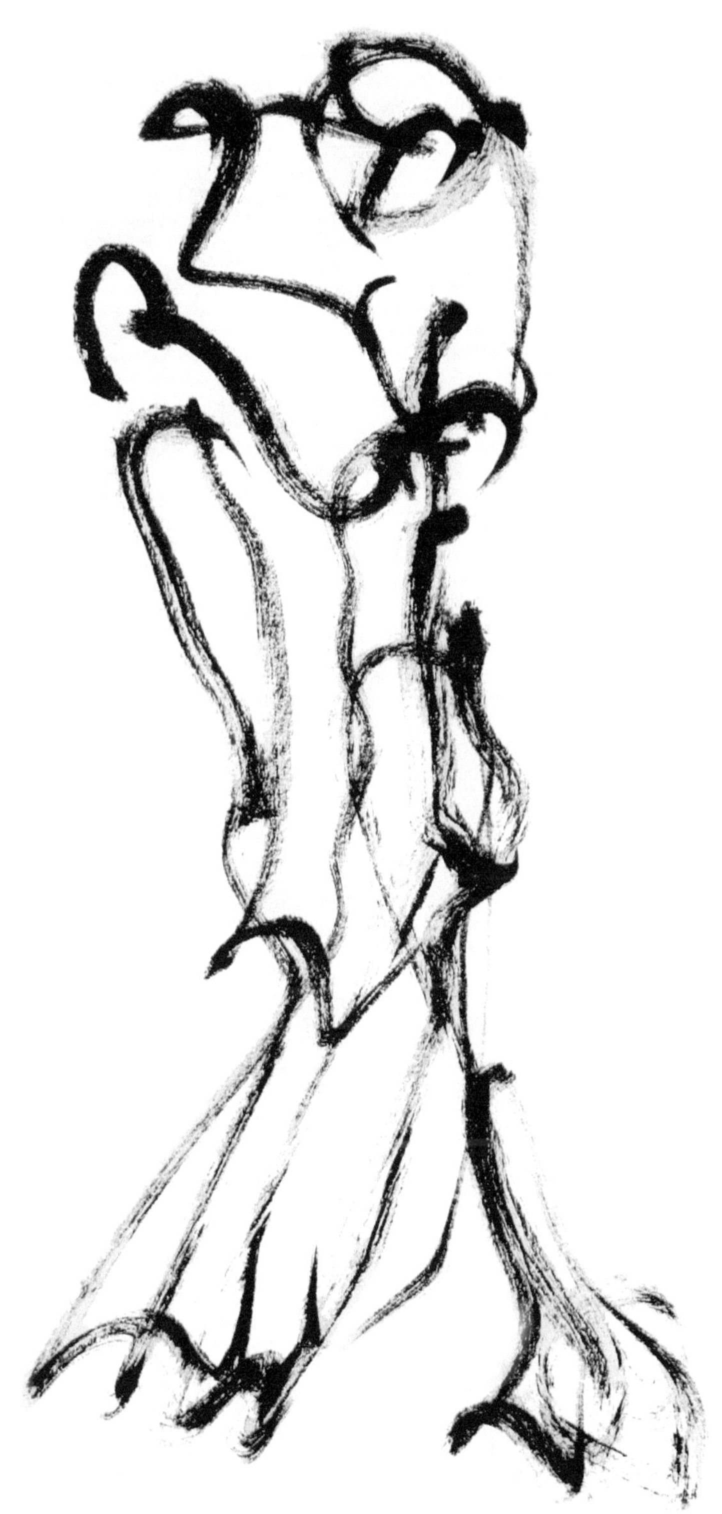

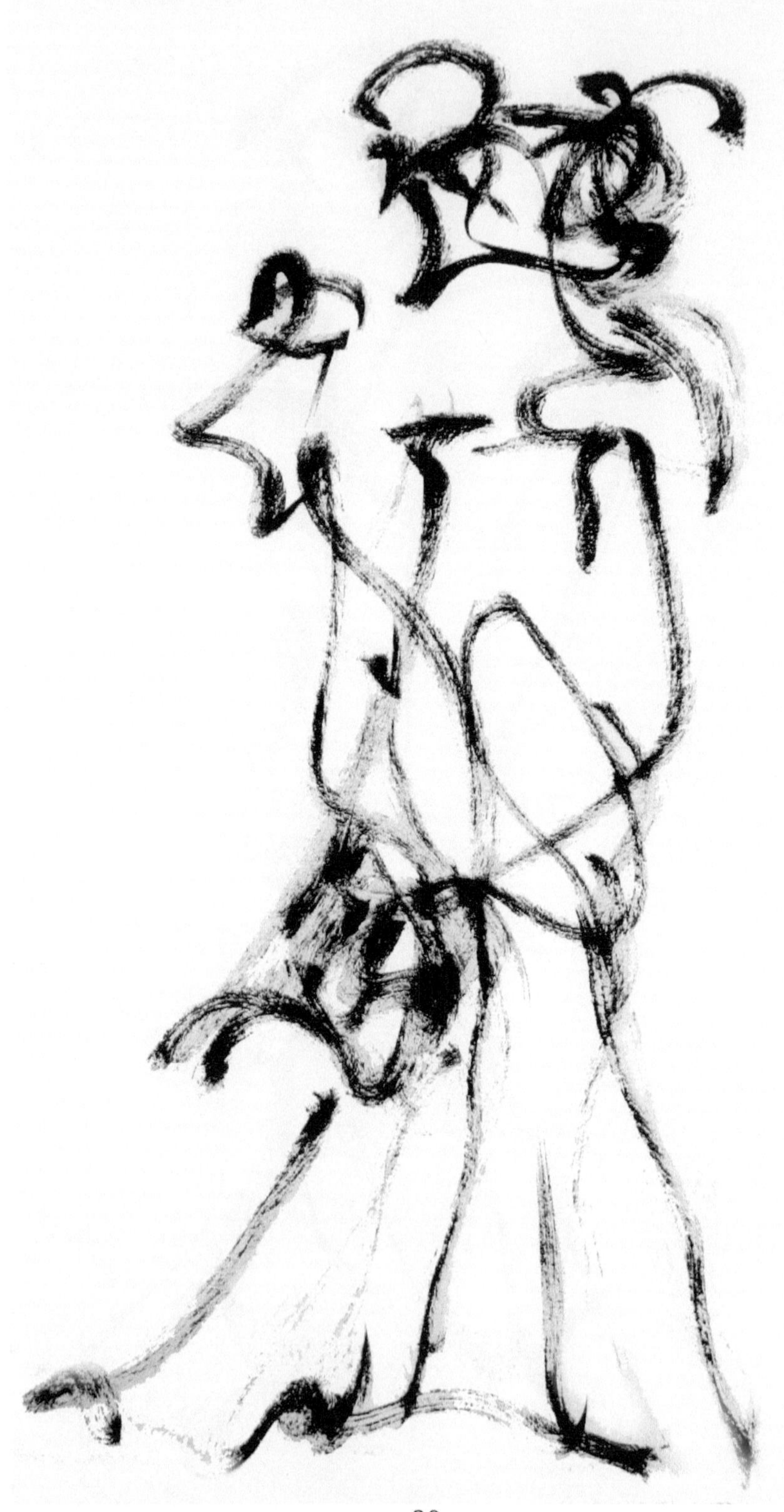

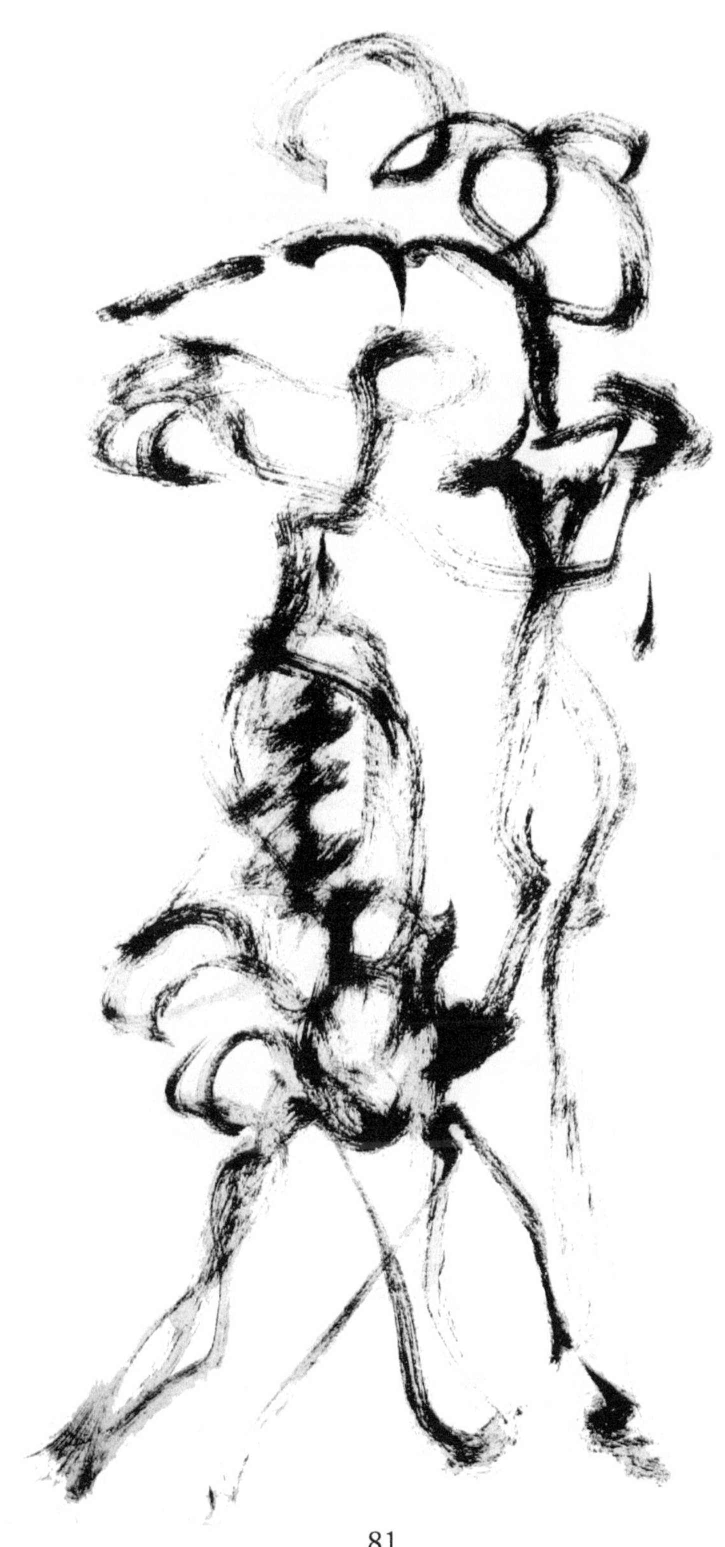

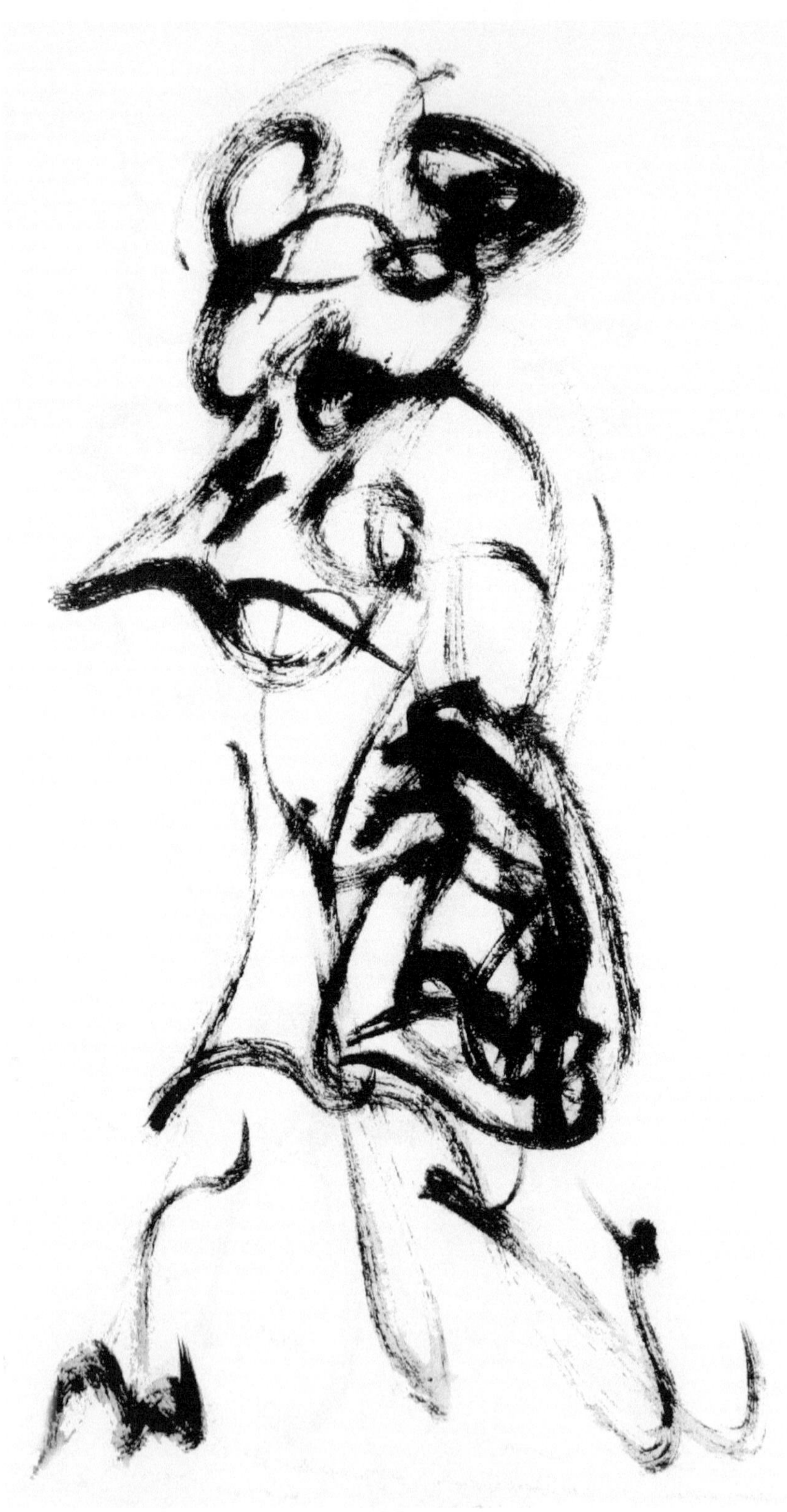

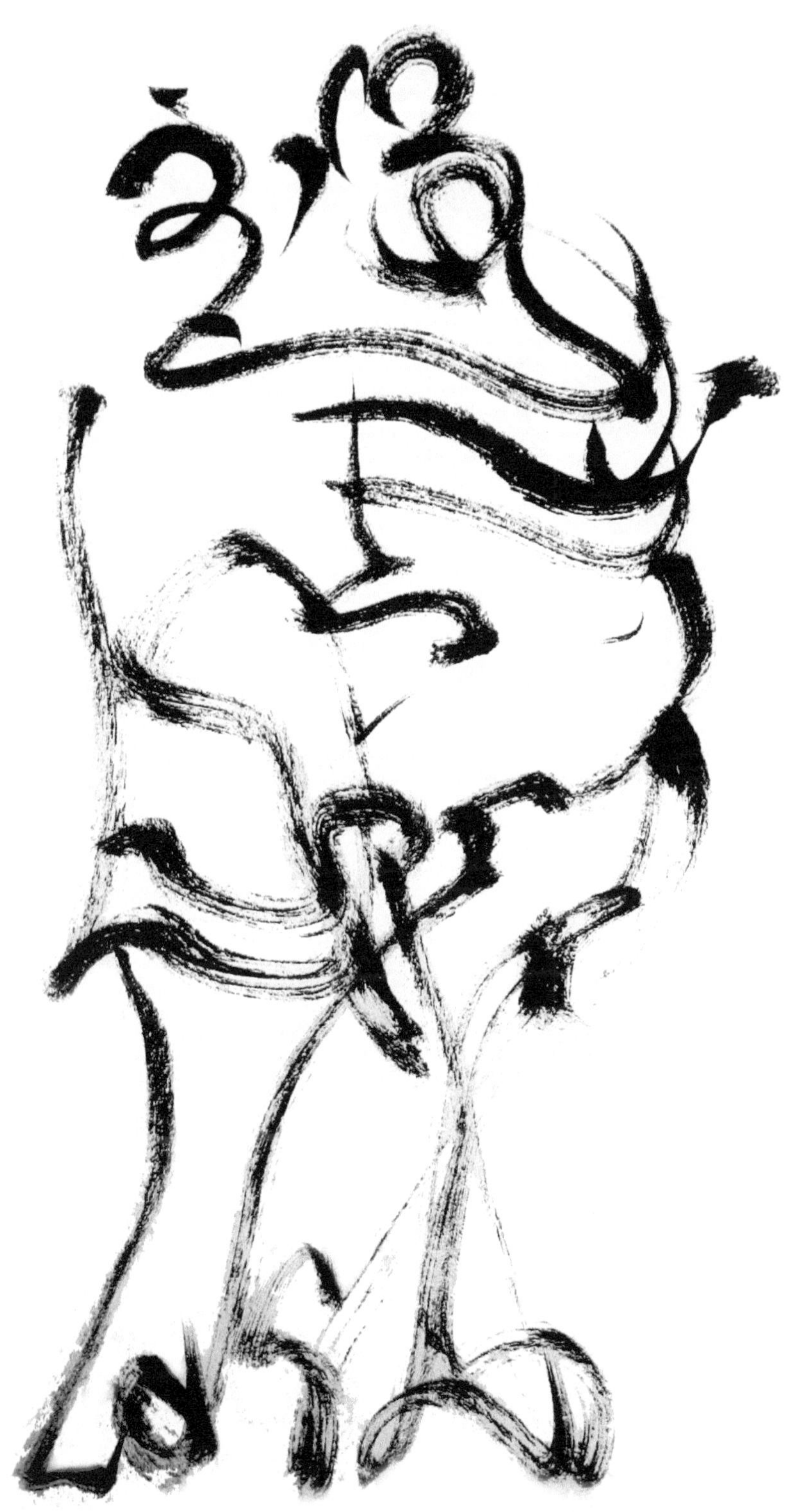

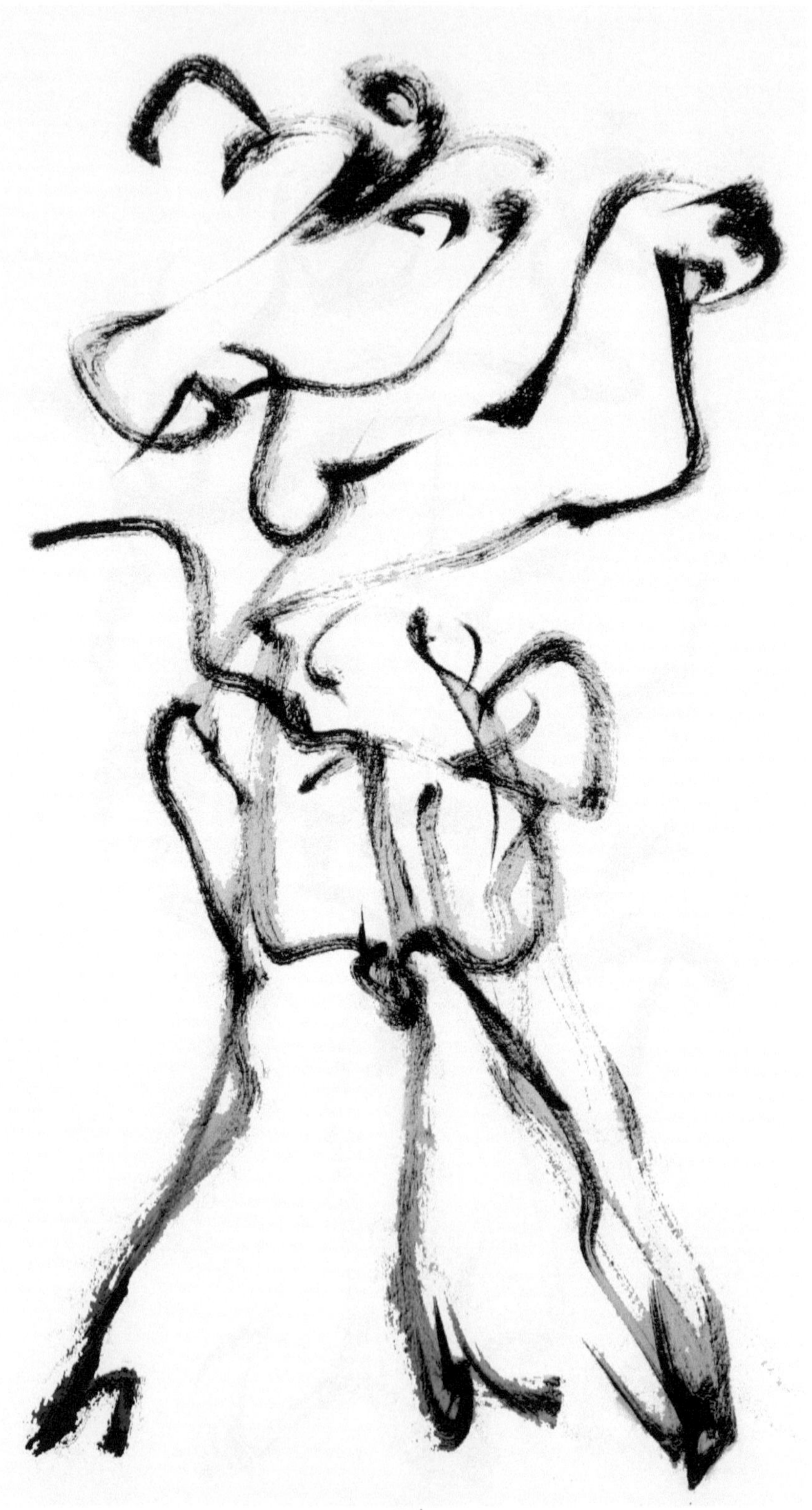

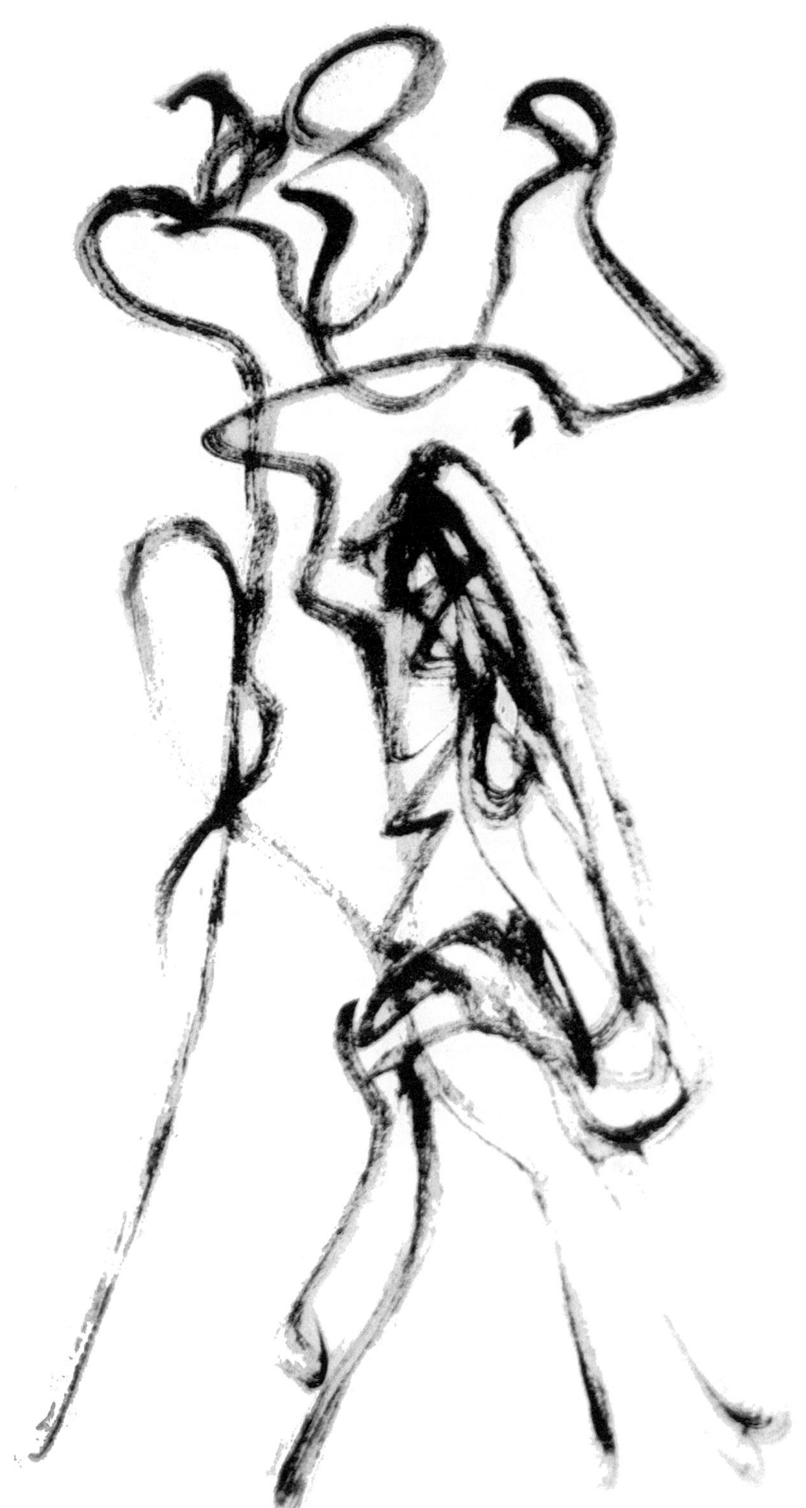

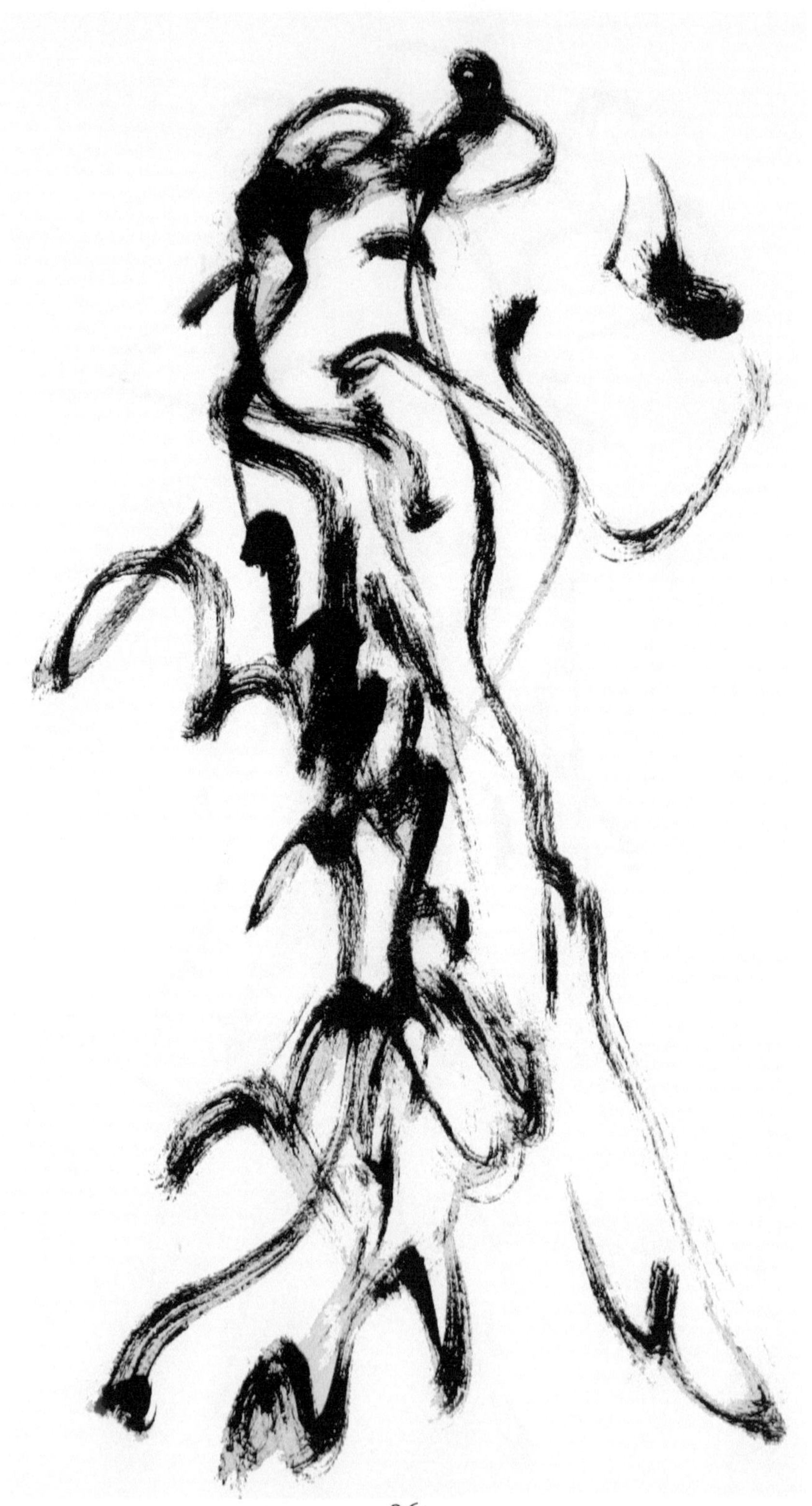

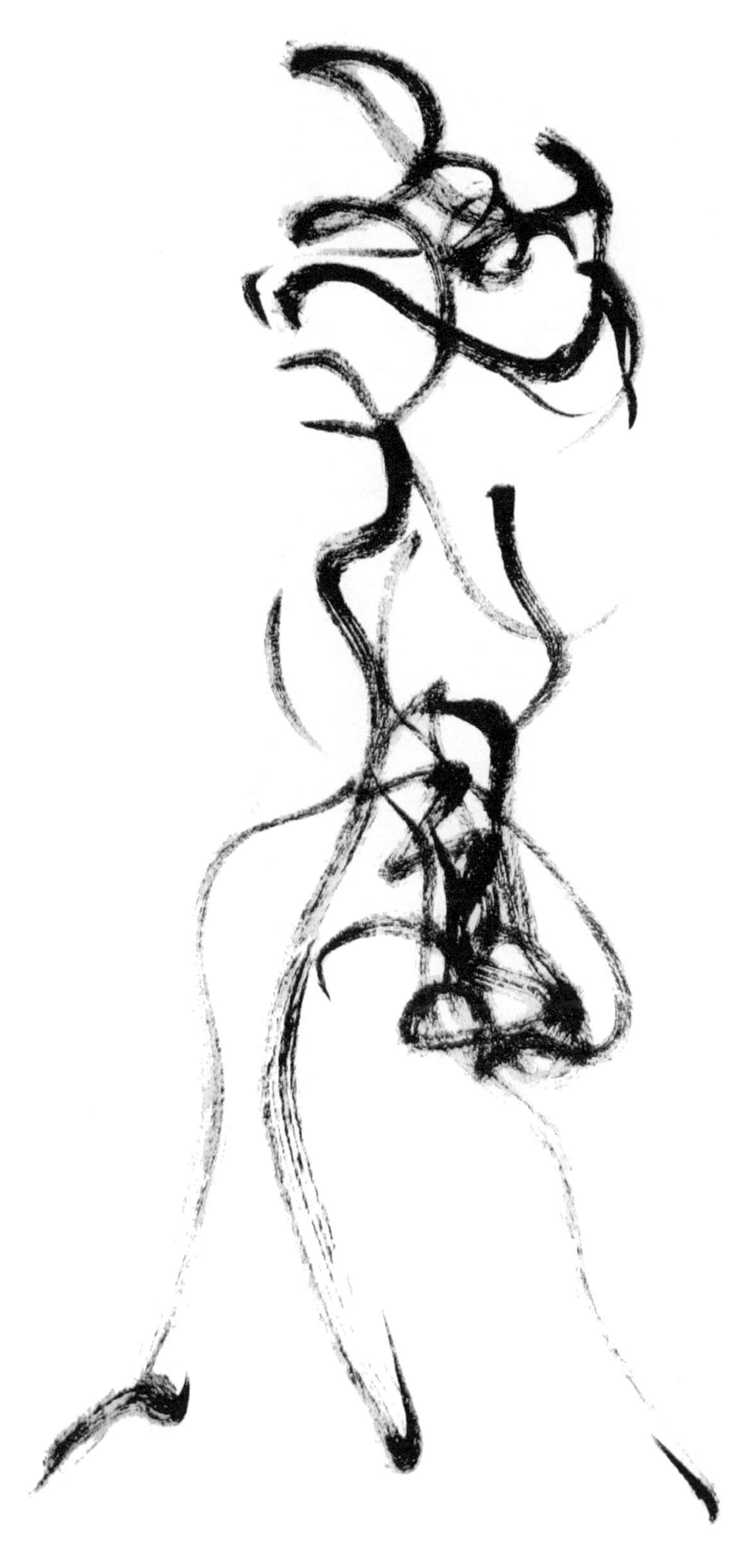

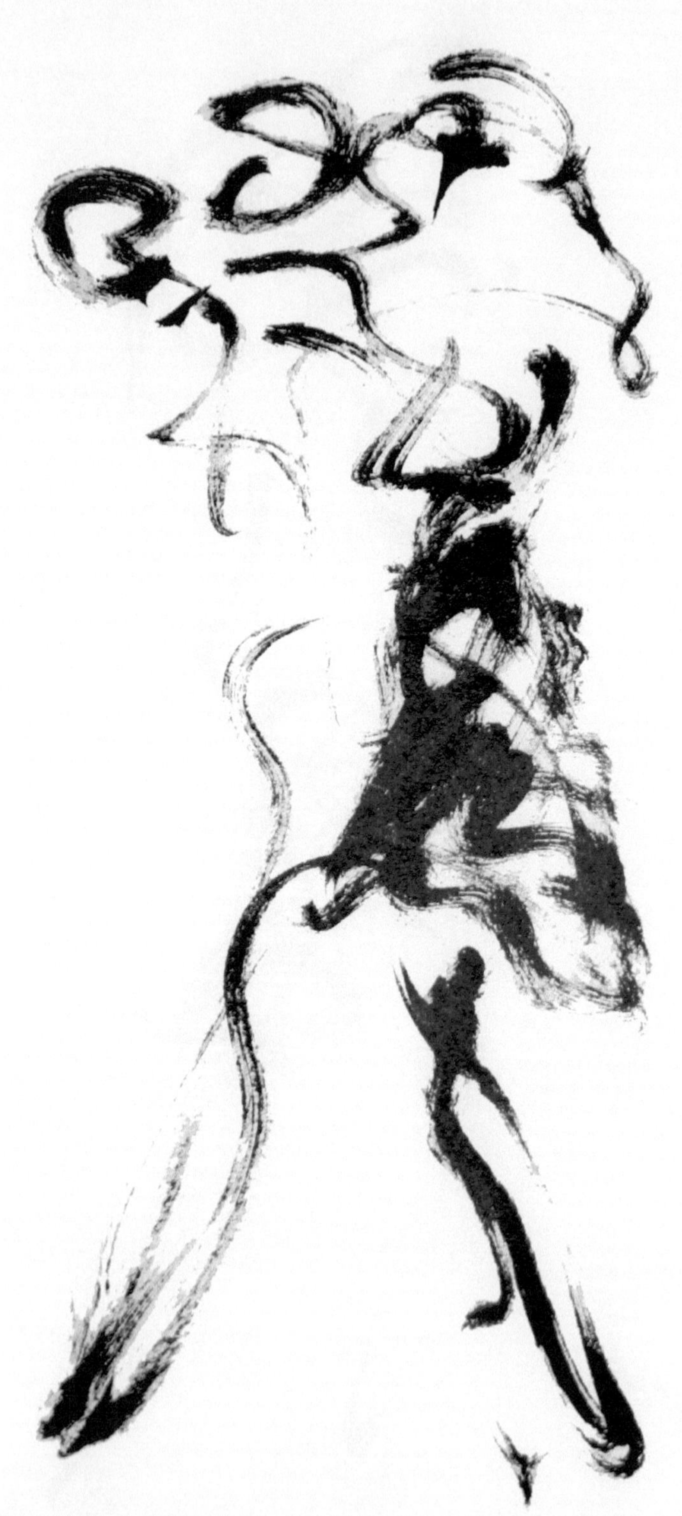

mountains moved to a tone

sands displaced to
music

i will not survive it

i have laughed for a century

i have also wept for
a century

i have drunk at your soul
enough to last me

for a century

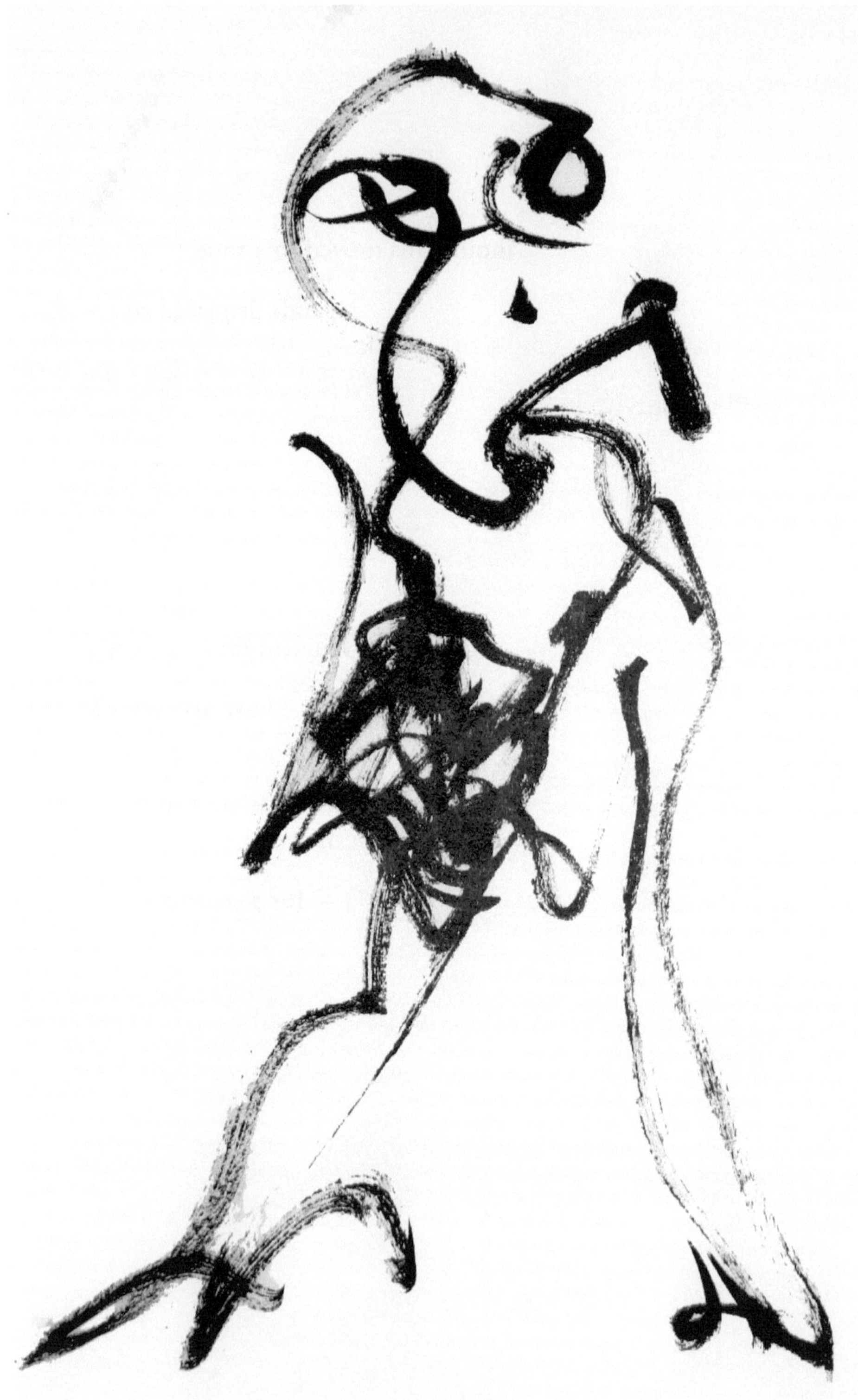

how many moons can one touch how many suns?

i used to think *this is only my body you can do anything you want* but this is not true

i used to say *this is only my body* but this not true

once you touch my body you also
touch my soul

time exists in infinitesimal degrees
filling up cracks where there is nothing

where there is nothing
there is time

transparent

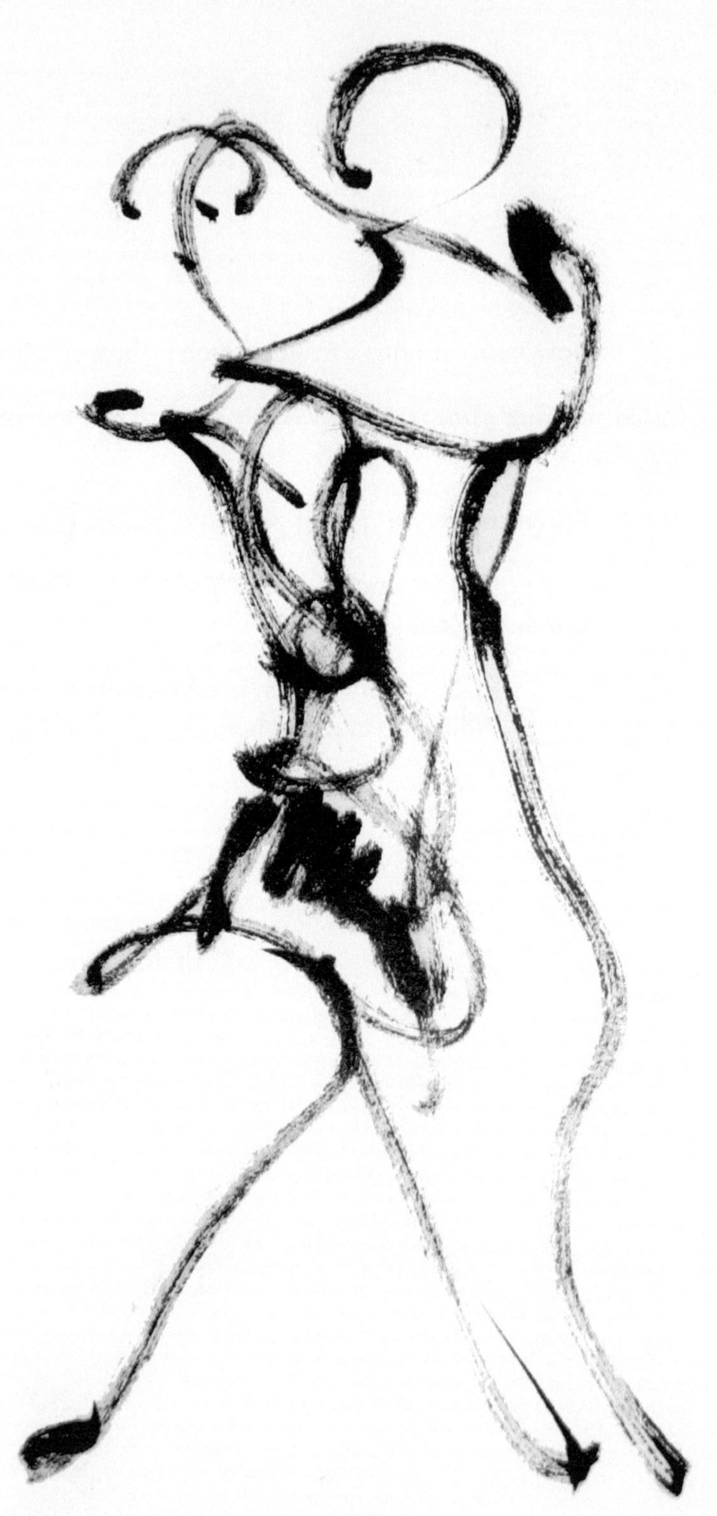

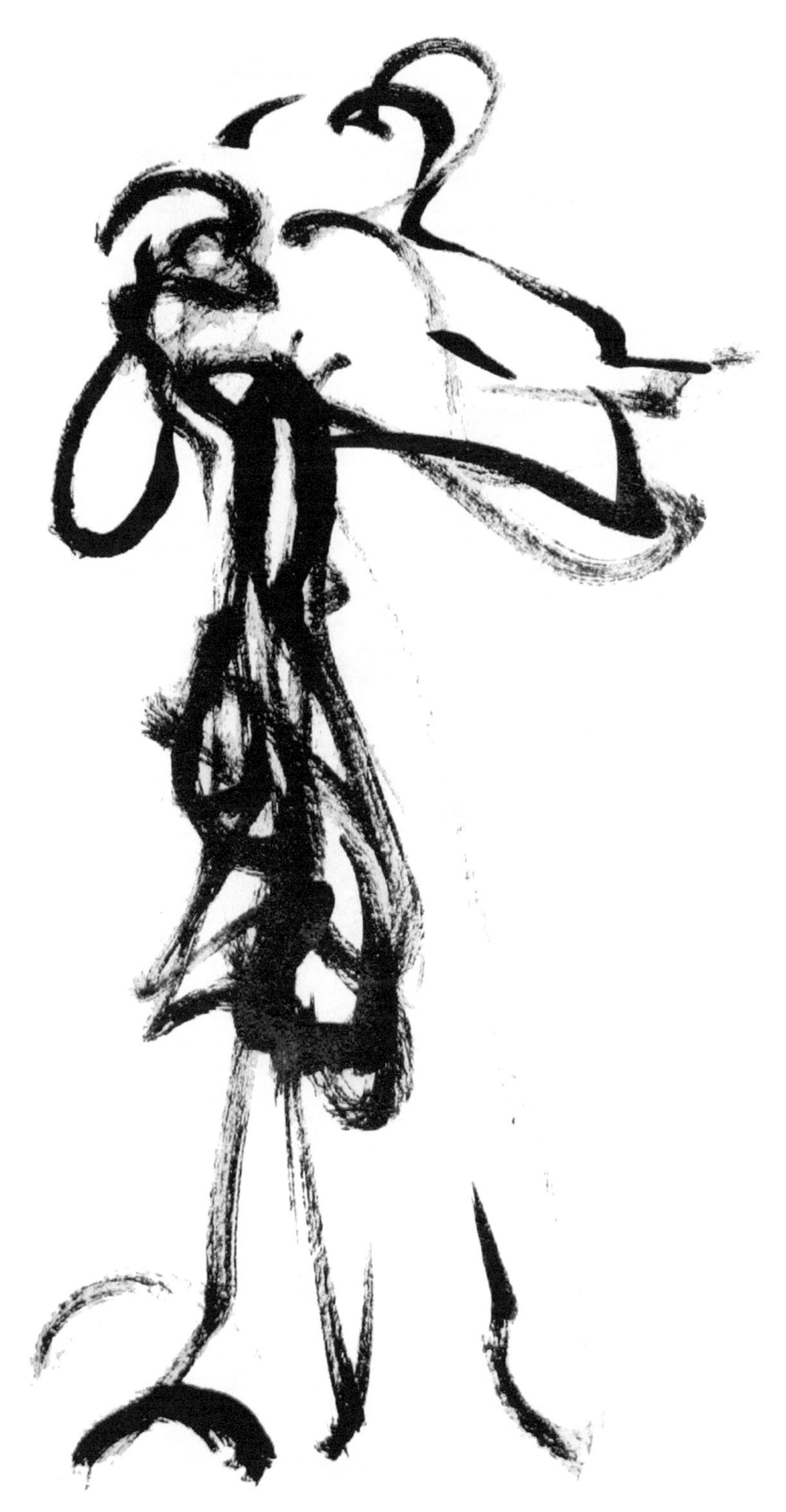

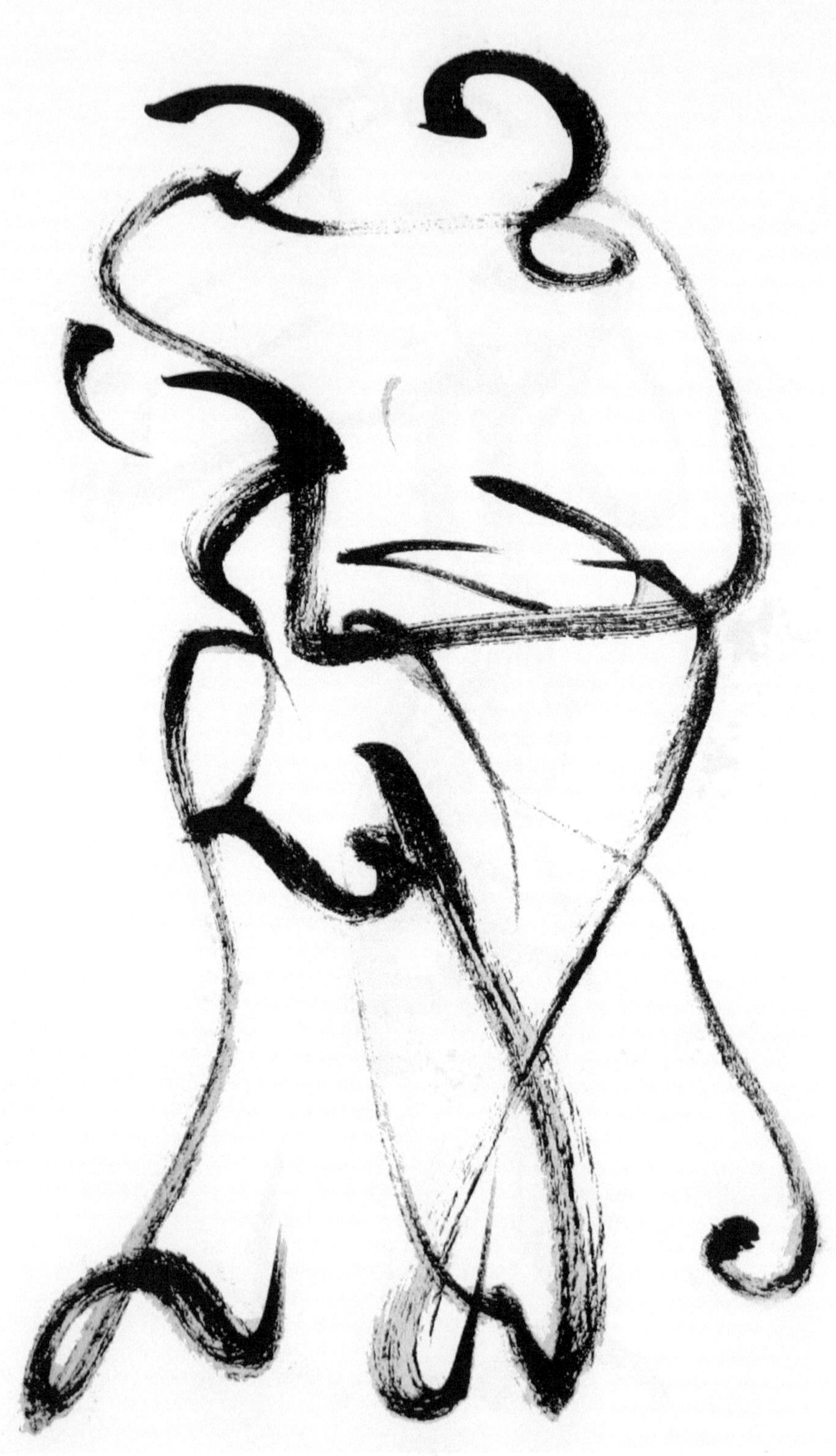

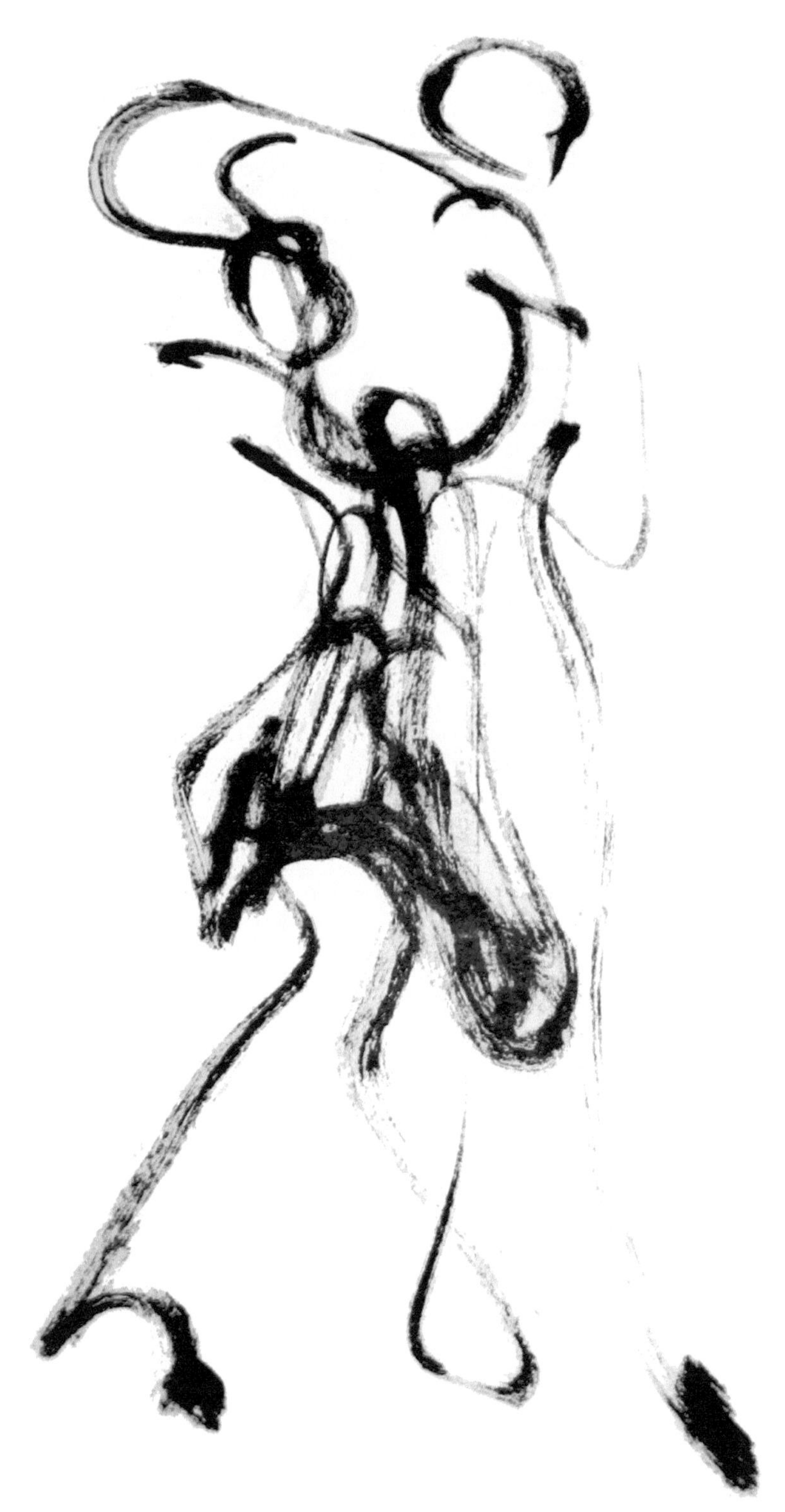

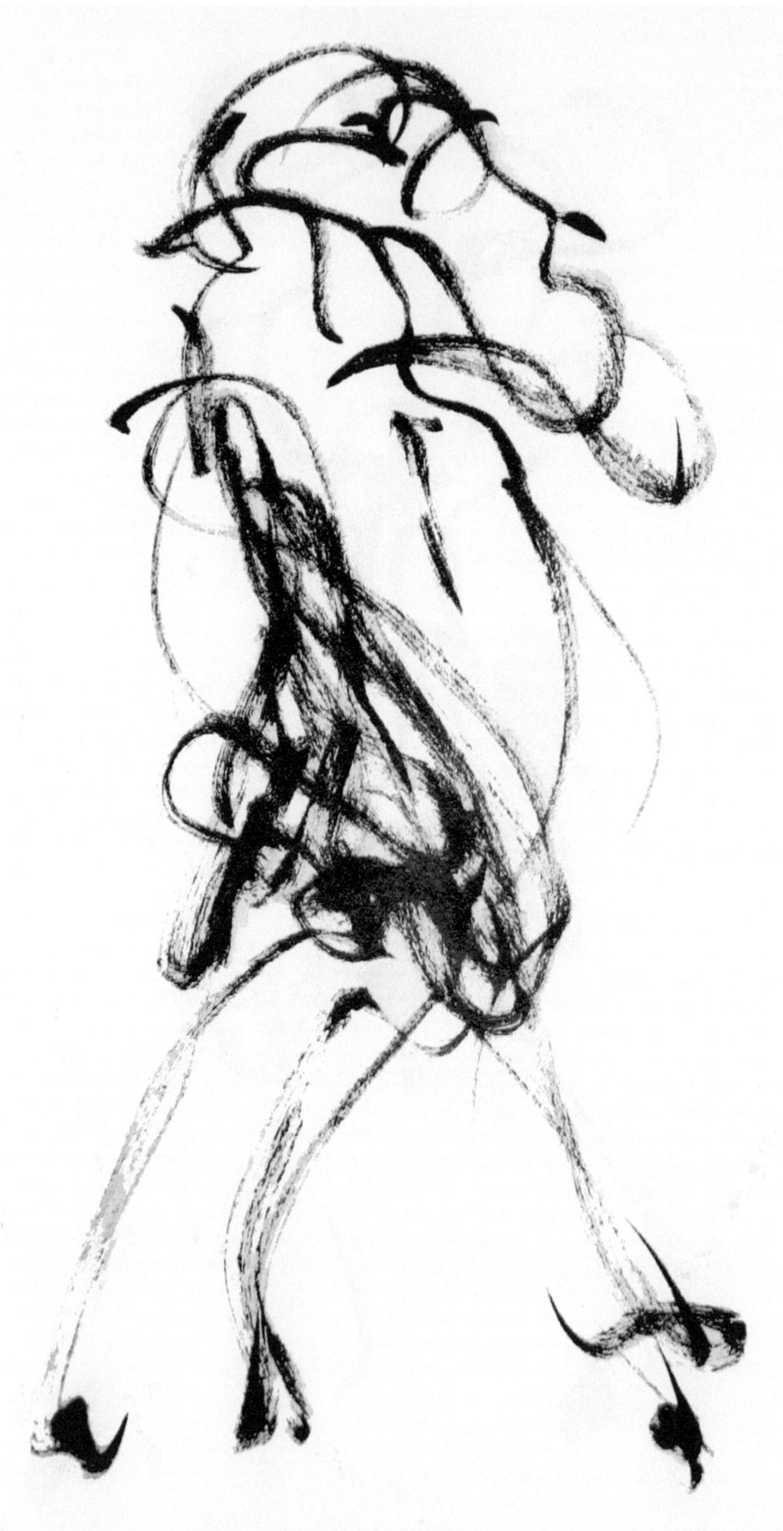

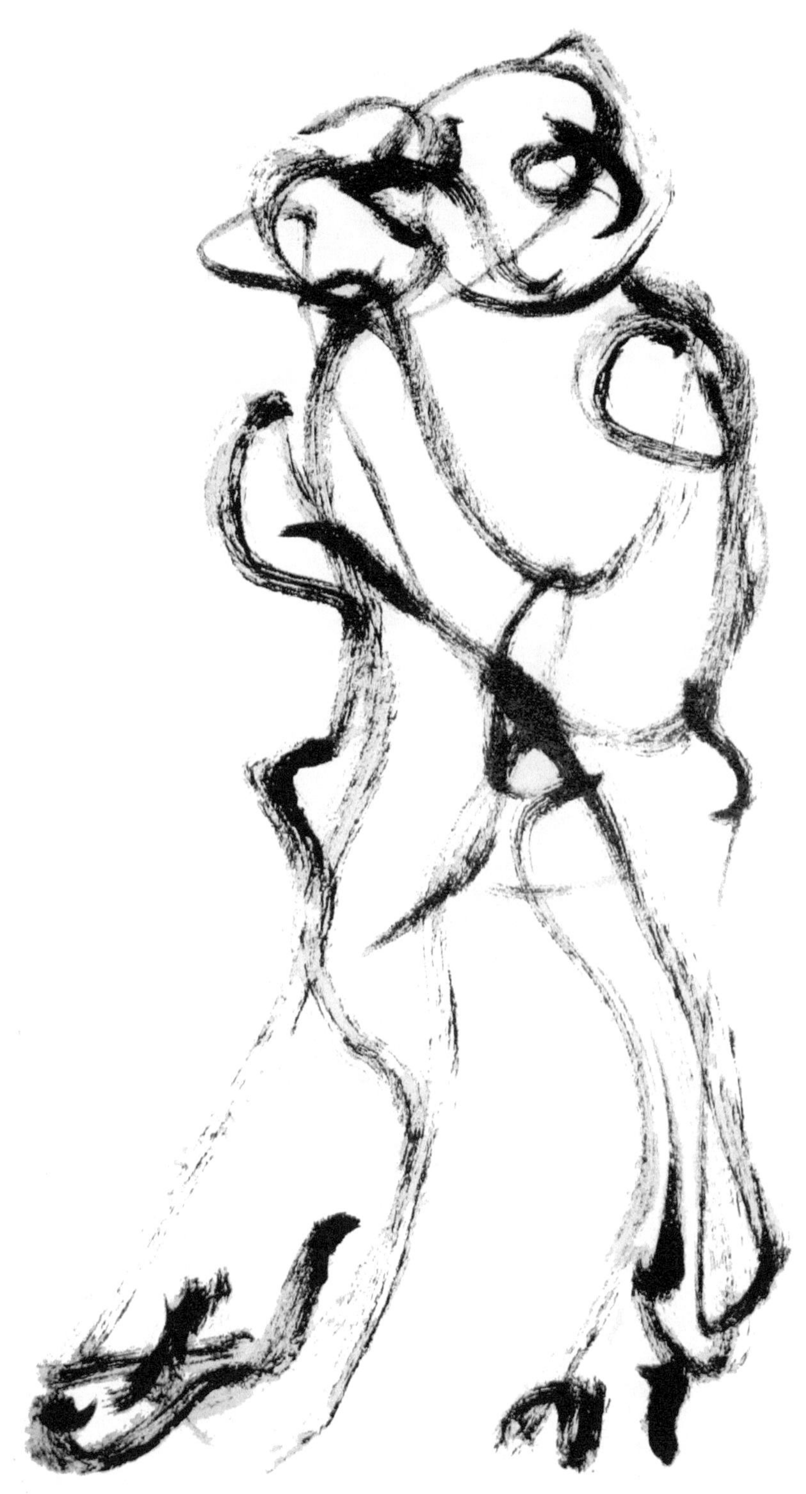

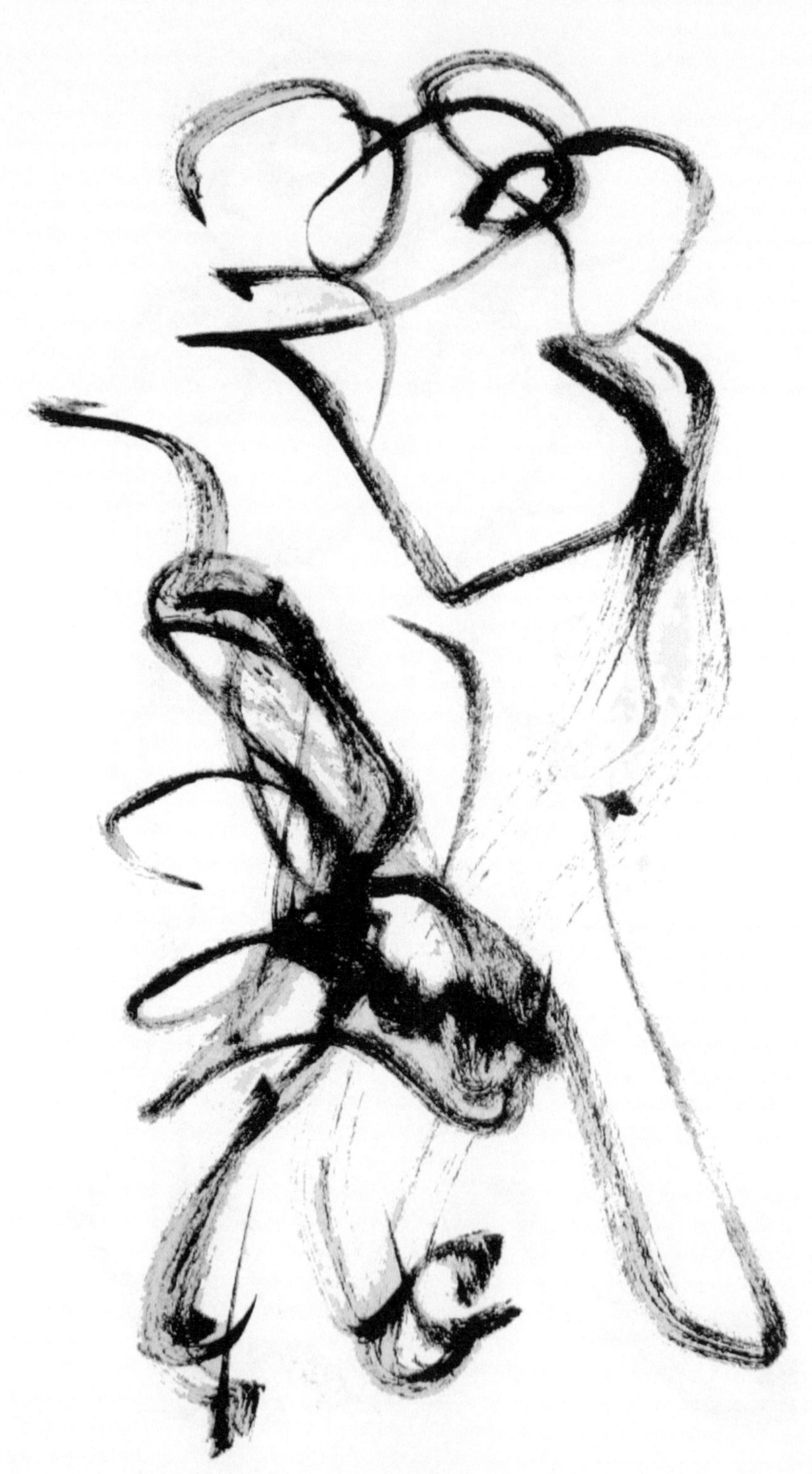

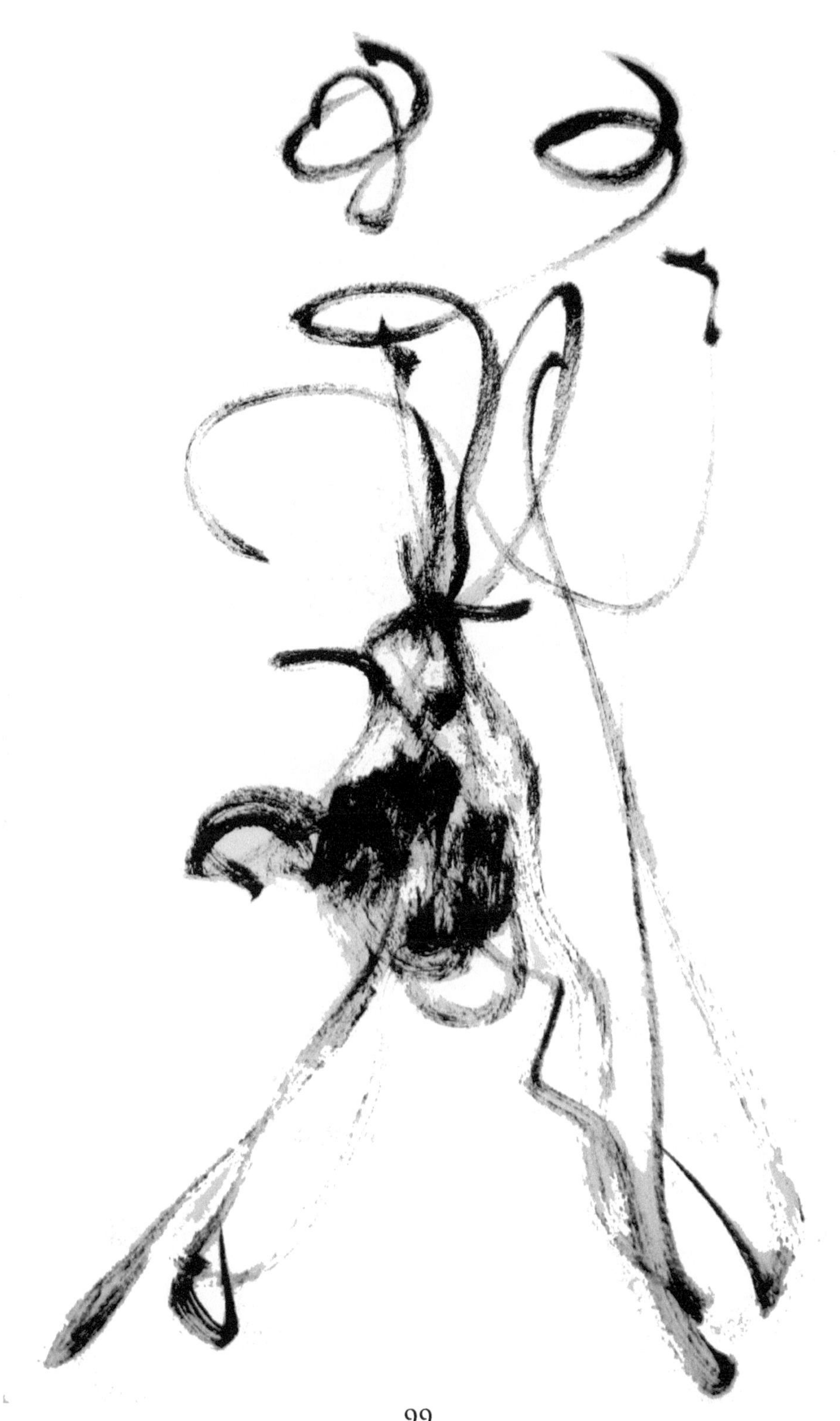

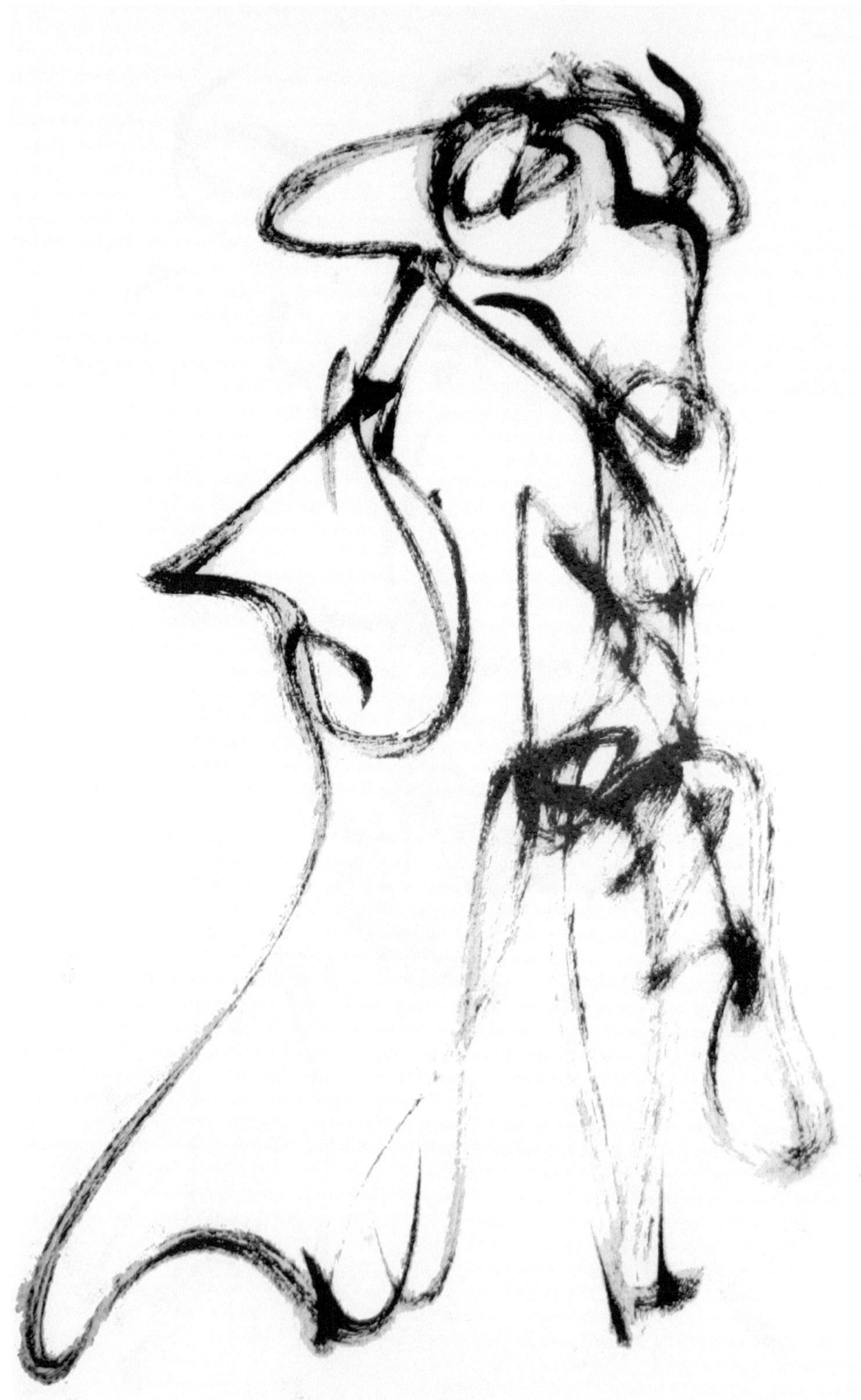

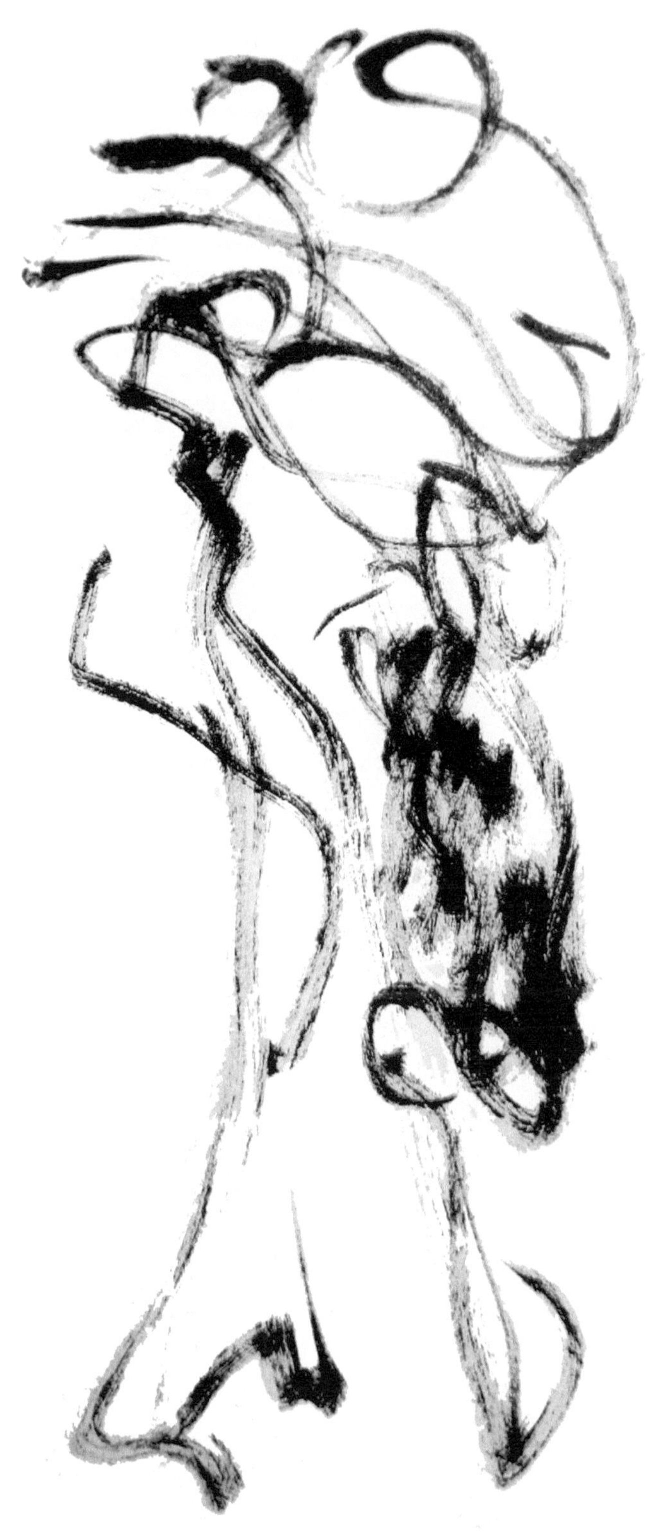

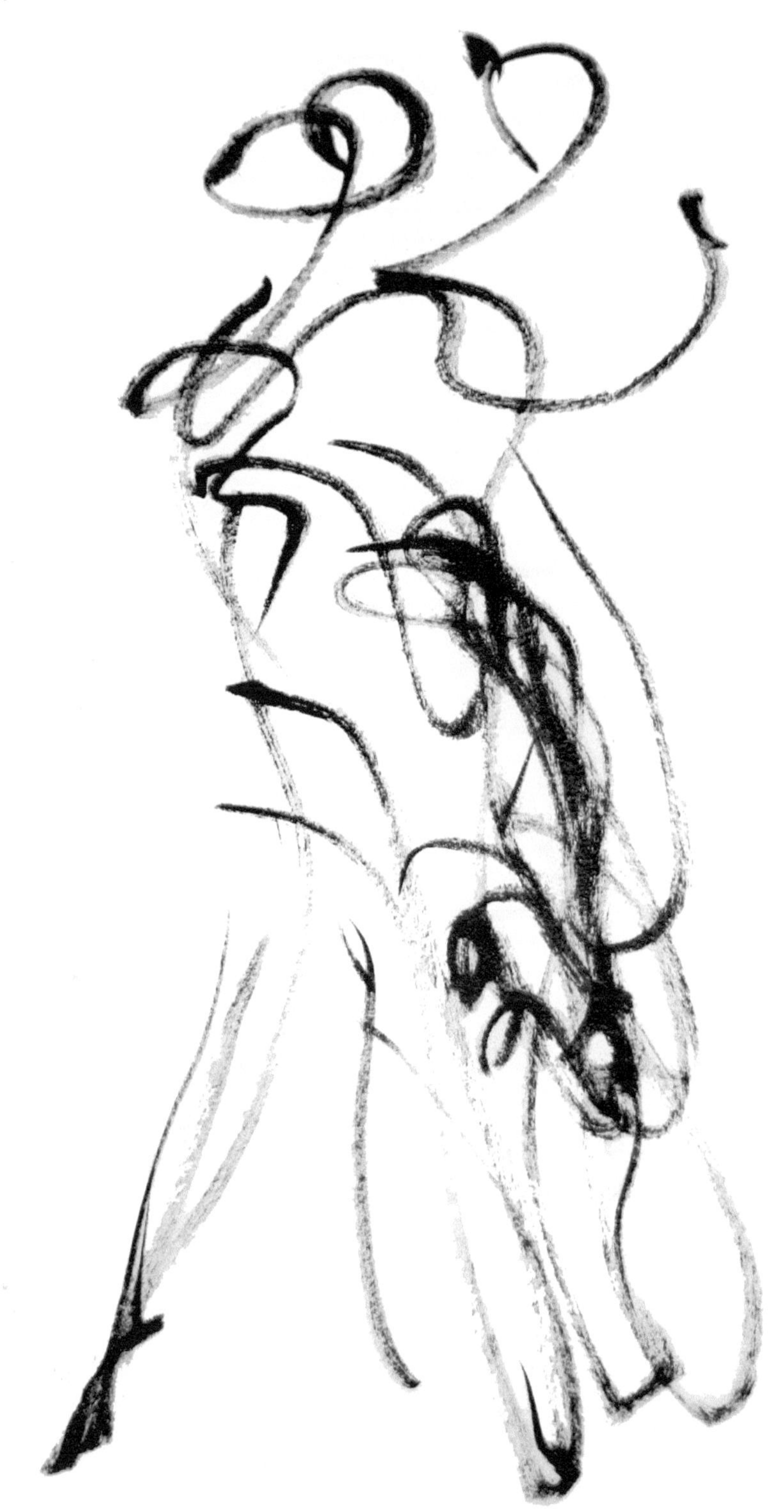

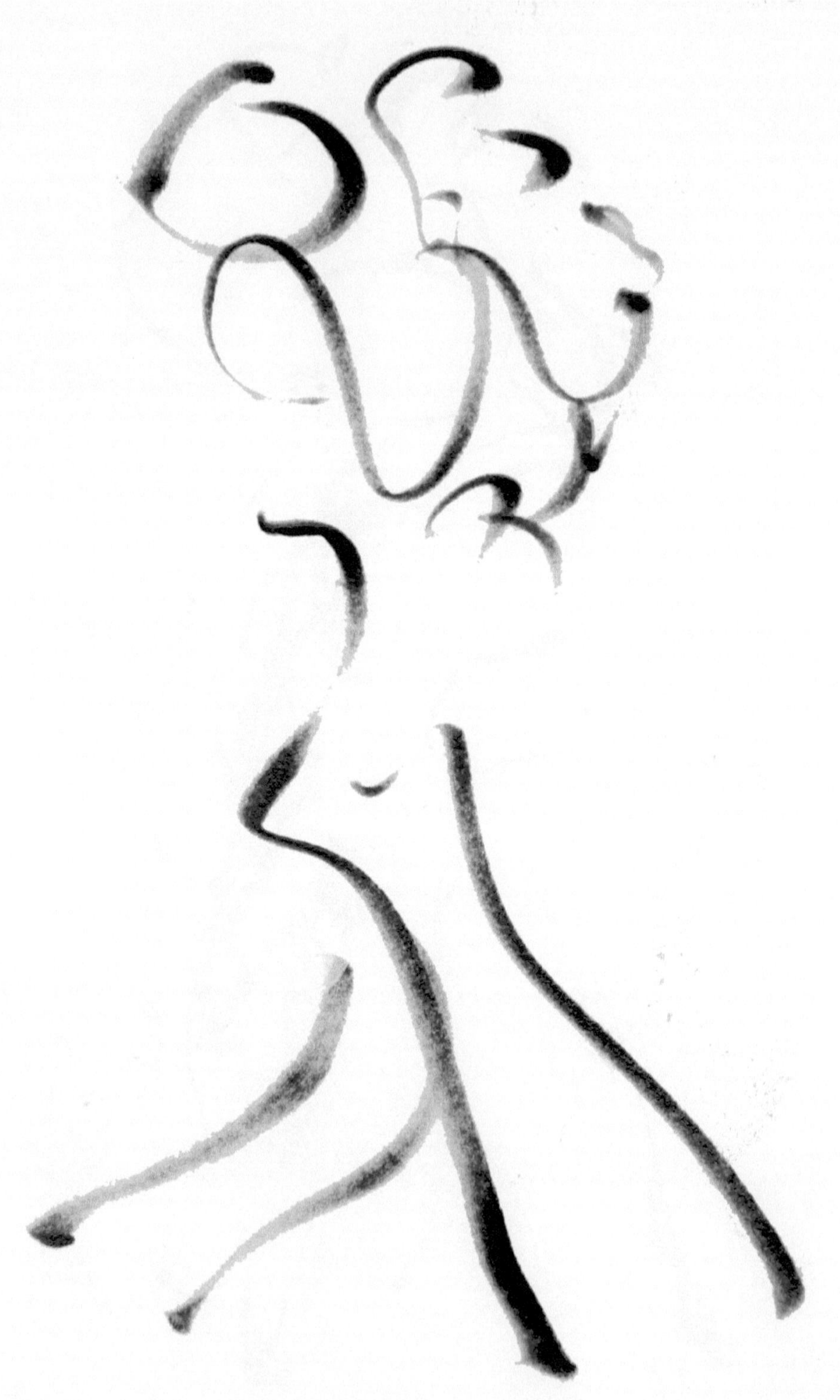

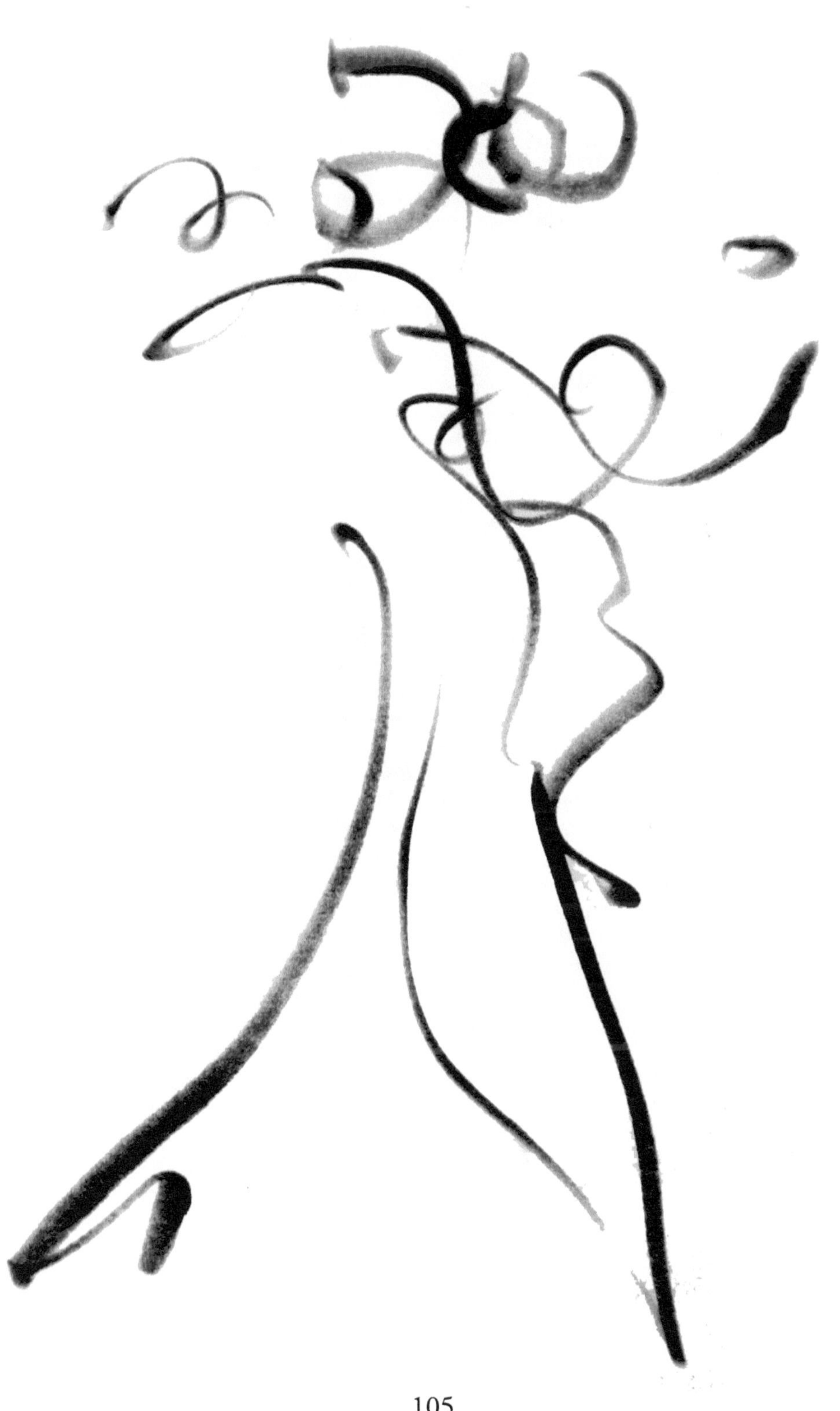

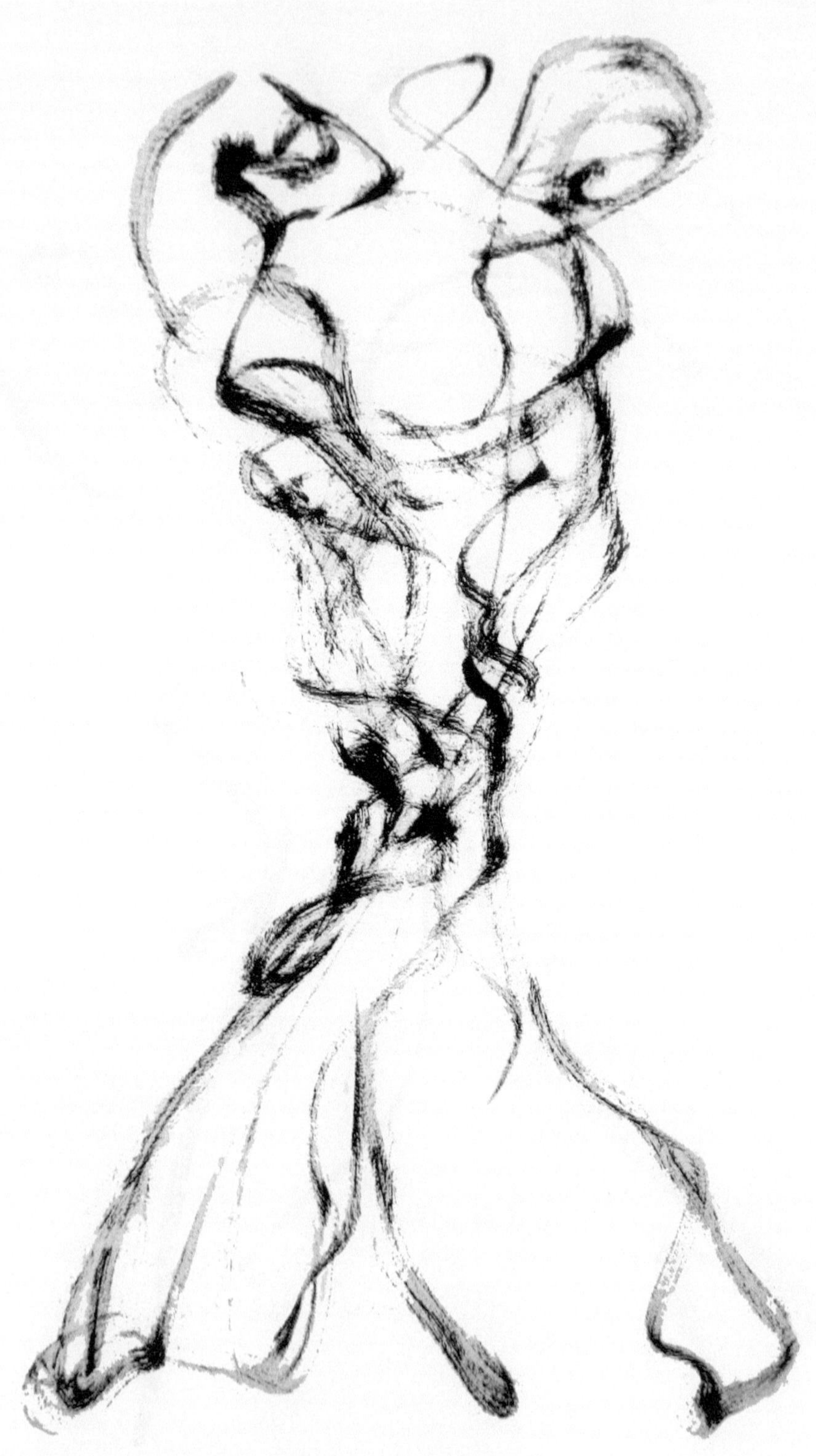

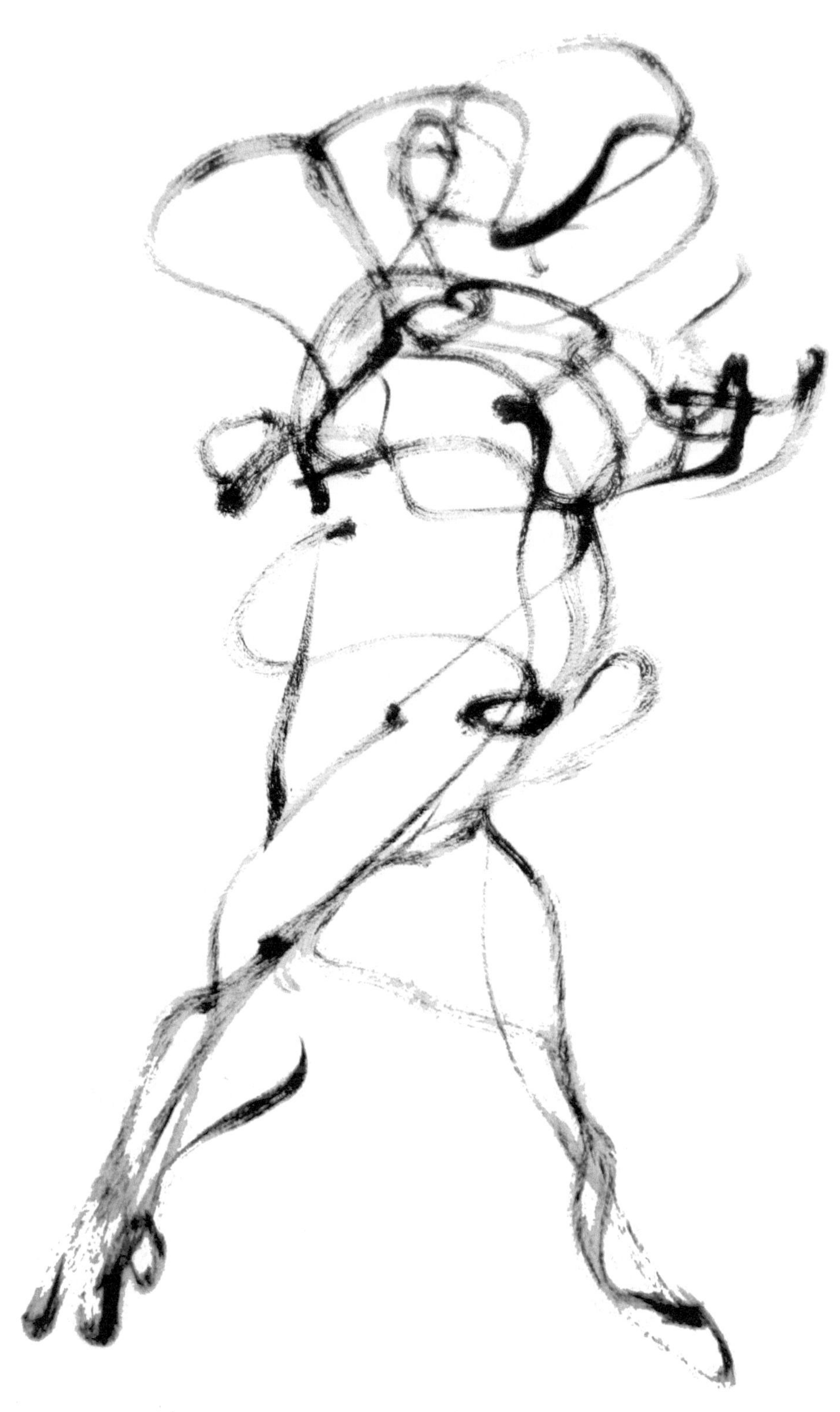

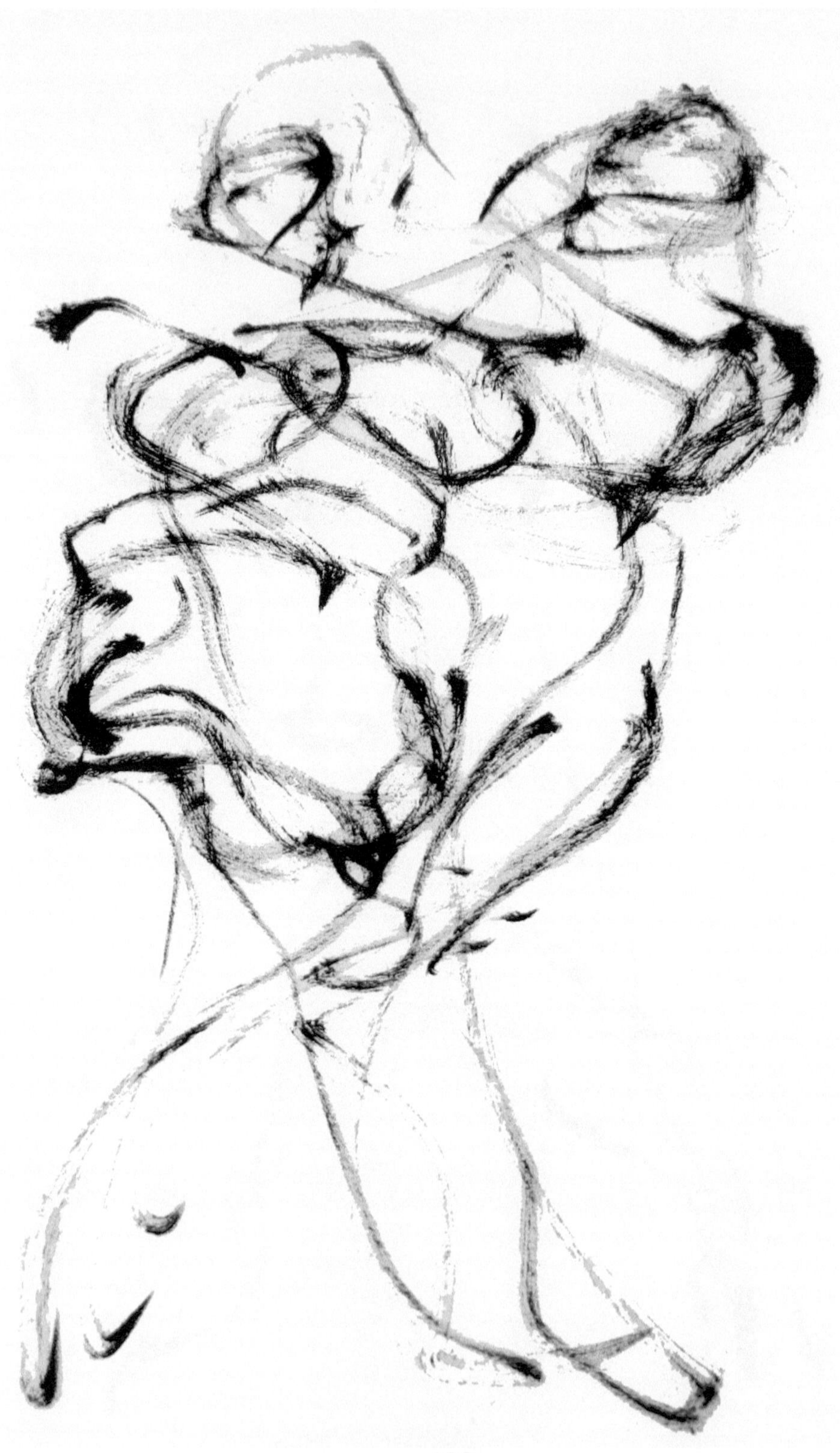

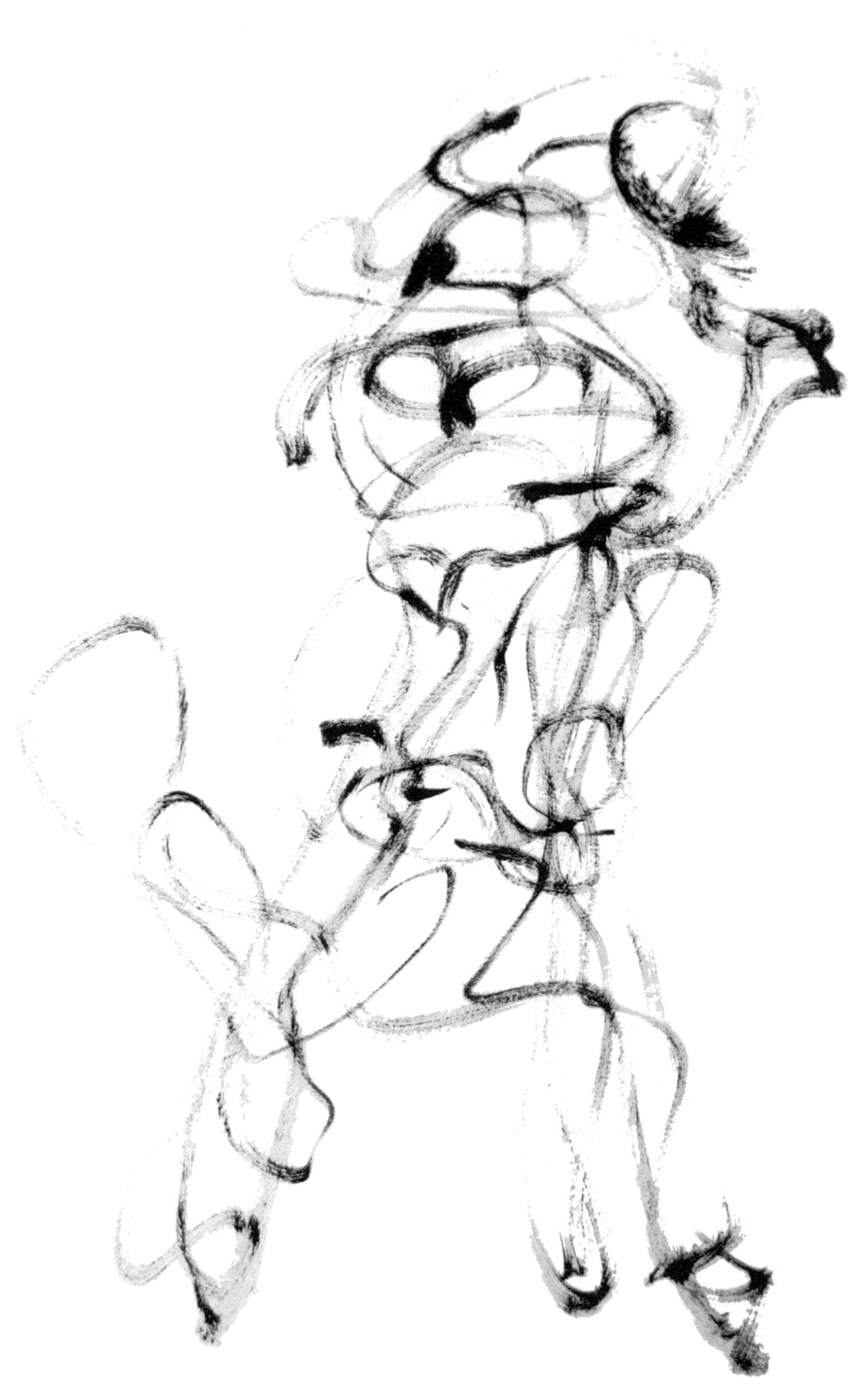

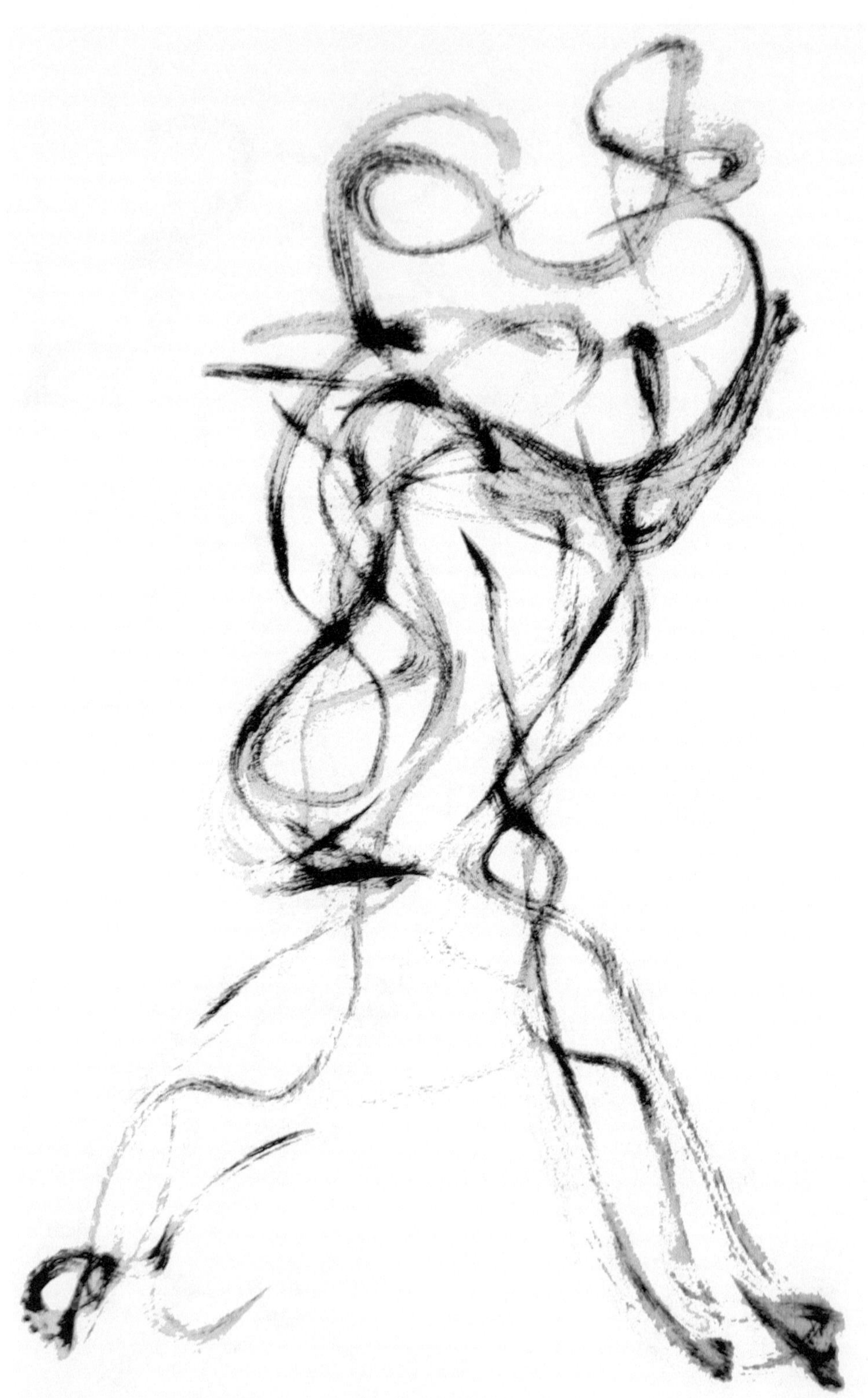

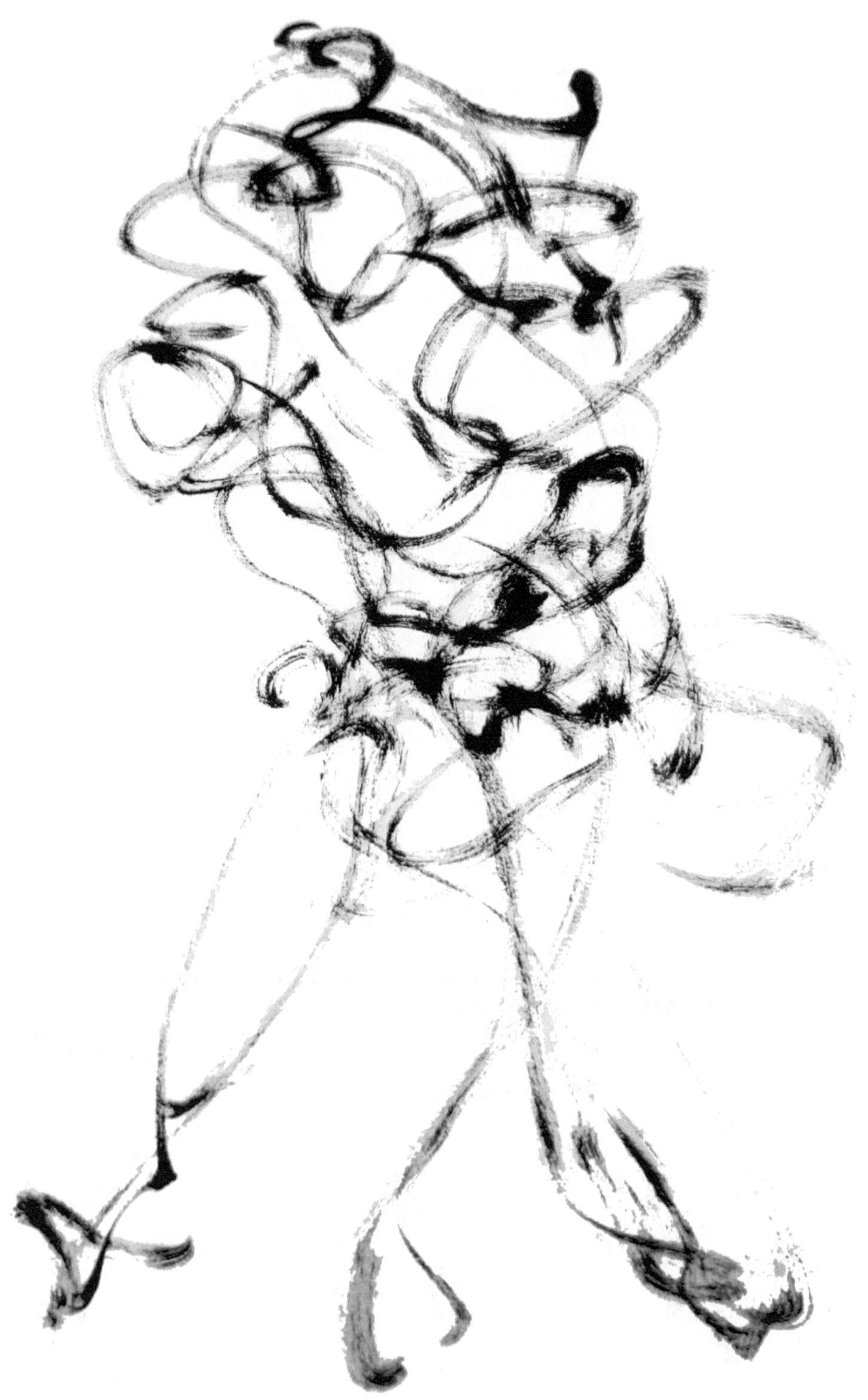

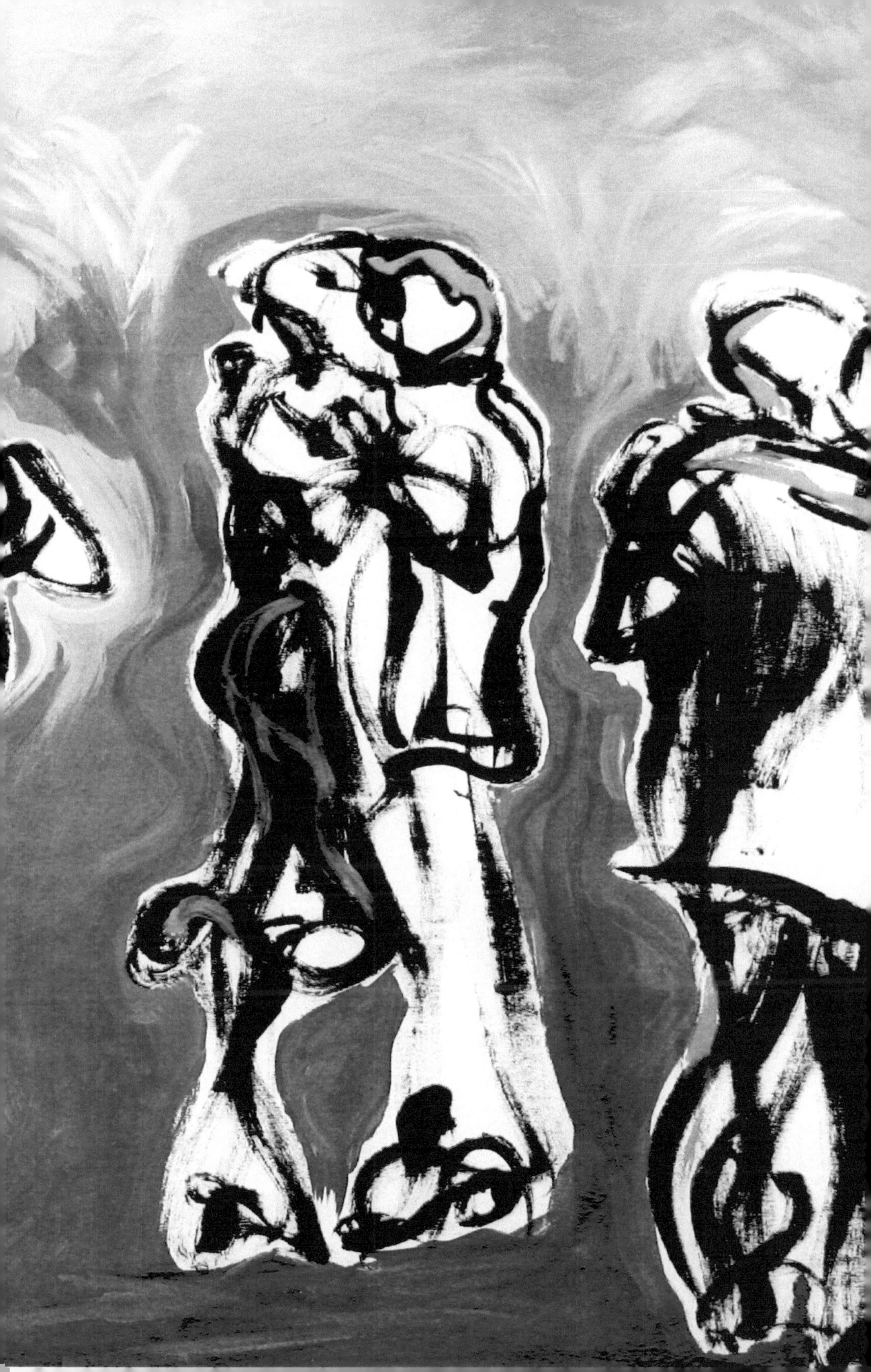

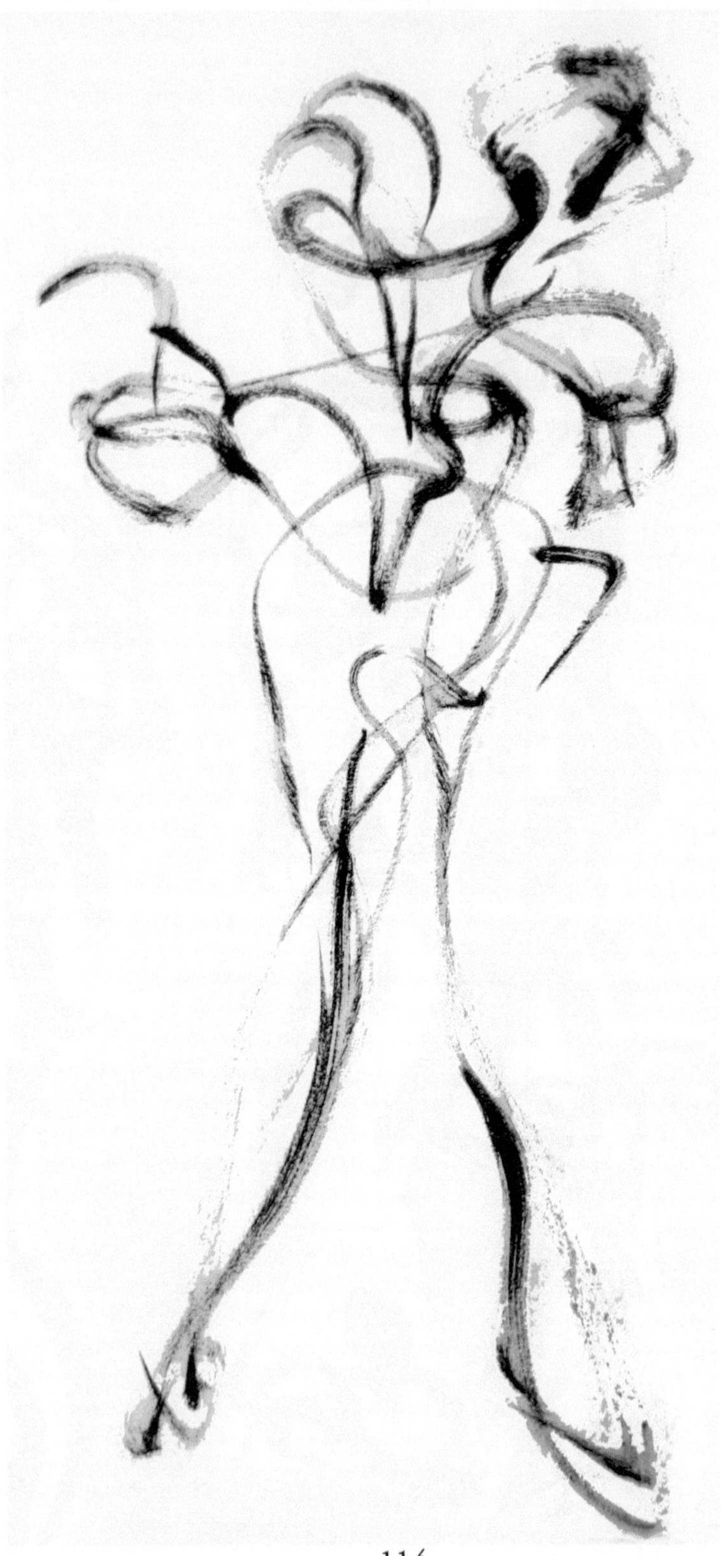

"ceniza del tiempo la cita de abril"

last night   i had one last moment of sweet bitterness
with you

incandescent night of days
flaming sun of my nights

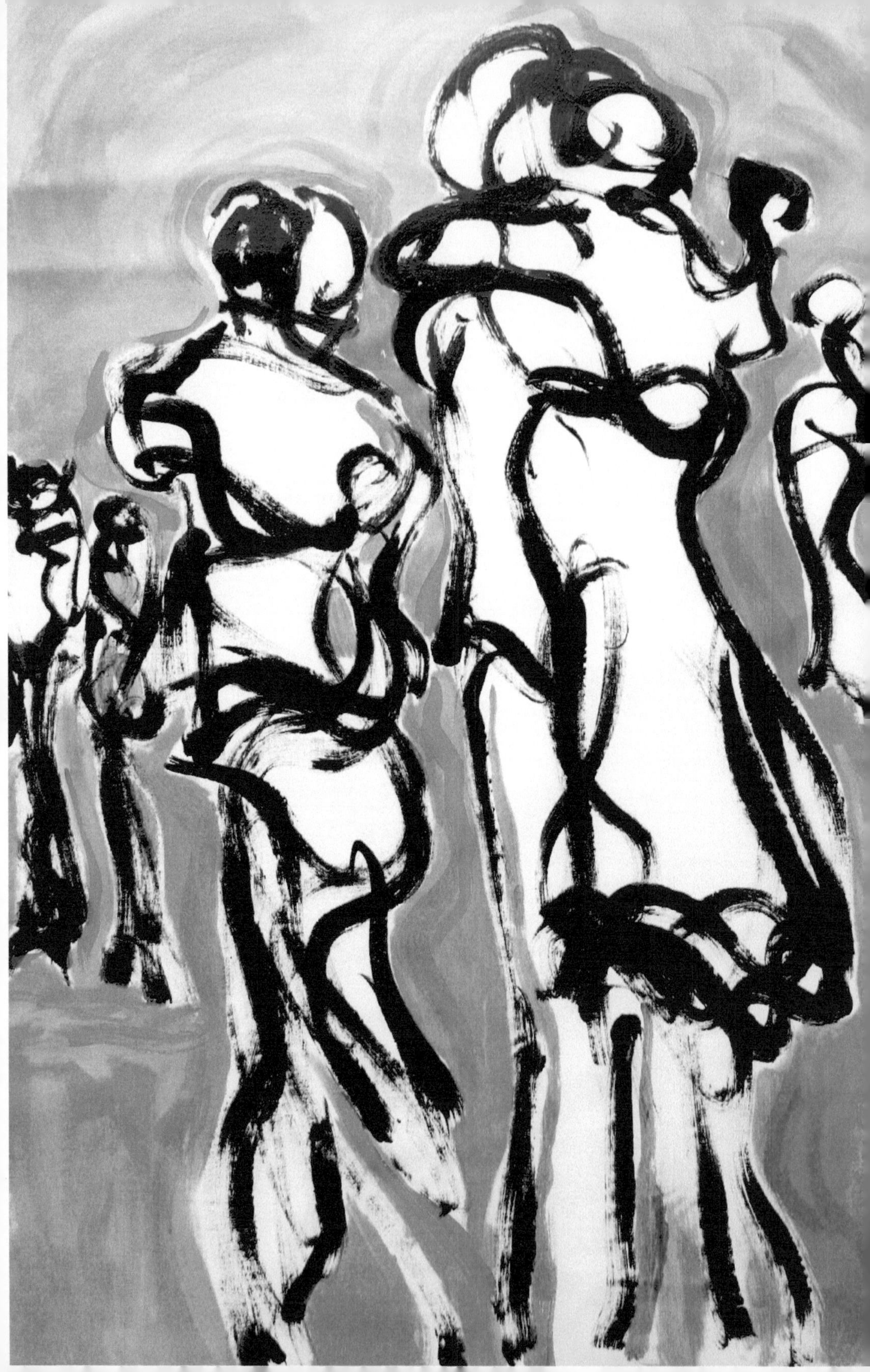

NOTES

The paintings and drawings in this book were done with Chinese and Japanese brush and ink on paper or canvas Sizes range from 20 cm x 30 cm to 110 cm x 110 cm.

Cover painting, *Tango in Red*, acrylic on canvas, 70 cm x 100 cm, 2011

Pages 112 and 113, *The Fountain of Tango,* acrylic on canvas, 110 cm x 110 cm, 2010.

Page 116, *Bodies in Tango Time,* acrylic on canvas, 70 cm x 100 cm, 2010.

~

My appreciation to the following sources, from which lines from tangos are quoted:

Page 9: Contursi, José María. "Como Dos Extraños." Editorial Musical Korn - Intersong S.A.I.C., Buenos Aires, 1940.

Page 61: Cadicamo, Enrique. "Nostalgias." http://www.todotango.com/Spanish/las_obras/Tema.aspx?id=Cl0N8uq82IU=

Page 74: Manzi, Homero. "Sur." Warner Chappell Music Argentina S.A.I.C., 1958.

Page 115: Manzi, Homero. "Romance de Barrio." A.U.R.A., 1947.

~

Loving thanks to my parents and family for your support over the years. Special thanks to Peter Hall and JA for your input. This book is dedicated to my sister Rose, past, present and future, and to all your loving ways.

ABOUT THE AUTHOR

Painter, photographer, poet, writer, educator and Argentine tango dancer, Mộng-Lan left her native Vietnam on the last day of the evacuation of Saigon. While still in high school, Mộng-Lan received scholarships to attend the Glassell School of Art in Houston for three years. Subsequently, her paintings and photographs have been exhibited for one year in the Capitol House in Washington D.C., in galleries in the United States, the Museum of Fine Arts in Houston, at the Dallas Museum of Art, and in public exhibitions in Buenos Aires, Bali, Bangkok, Seoul and Tokyo. In conjunction with the National Endowment for the Arts, she was the Dallas Museum of Fine Arts' inaugural Visual Artist and Poet in Residence in 2005. An exhibition of her paintings and photographs, "The World of Mộng-Lan," ran for six months at the Museum.

Mộng-Lan's first book of poems, *Song of the Cicadas,* was awarded the Juniper Prize (UMASS Press) and the 2002 Great Lakes Colleges Association's New Writers Awards for Poetry, and also was a finalist for the Poetry Society of America's Norma Farber Award. Her other books include *Why is the Edge Always Windy?*; *Tango, Tangoing: Poems & Art;* the bilingual Spanish-English edition, *Tango, Tangueando: Poemas & Dibujos;* and *Love Poem to Tofu & Other Poems* (chapbook), the latter of which includes her pen & ink art as well. Mộng-Lan's poetry has been widely anthologized to include being in *Best American Poetry*; *The Pushcart Book of Poetry: Best Poems from 30 Years of the Pushcart Prize*; *Asian American Poetry: the Next Generation*; *Language for a New Century: Contemporary Poetry from the Middle East, Asia, and Beyond* (Norton); *Force Majeure* (Indonesia); *Black Dog, Black Night: Contemporary Vietnamese Poetry*; and *Jungle Crows: a Tokyo Expatriate anthology*; and has appeared in leading American literary journals.

A Wallace E. Stegner Fellow in poetry for two years at Stanford University and a Fulbright Fellow in Vietnam, Mộng-Lan took her Master of Fine Arts at the University of Arizona. She has taught at Stanford University, the University of Arizona, and the University of Maryland in Tokyo. She also has given scores of readings and academic presentations in the United States, Argentina, Germany, Indonesia, Japan, Korea, Malaysia, Switzerland, Thailand, and Vietnam. Based in Buenos Aires, Mộng-Lan travels frequently to show her artwork, give readings and lectures, and to teach and dance tango. Visit: www.monglan.com

www.ingramcontent.com/pod-product-compliance
Ingram Content Group UK Ltd.
Pitfield, Milton Keynes, MK11 3LW, UK
UKHW041936190726
13854UKWH00004B/1624

9 780982 822708